Illustrated Masonic Secrets
of
America's Founding Fathers

Bottletree®

GREAT CONTENT. GREAT BOOKS.™

BottletreeBooks.com

Illustrated Masonic Secrets
of
America's Founding Fathers

Editors of Bottletree Books

First Edition
Manufactured in the United States
or the United Kingdom
ISBN: 978-1-933747-13-2

Printed on 100% recycled paper in both
the United States and United Kingdom
(20% Post Consumer Waste)

Font: Bookman Old Style

Copyrights: © Copyright Bottletree Books LLC, 2008. All rights reserved. Registered at the U.S. Copyright Office under Reg. No. TXu001573872. Digital images of the front and back covers may be resized and shown as "fair use" for purposes of selling and promoting the book. Copyright exists in the selection, coordination and arrangement of the text and images both individually and collectively.

Trademarks: BOTTLETREE, BOTTLETREE BOOKS, BottleTree Logo, and related trade dress, including all cover art designs are trademarks of Bottletree Books, LLC, and may not be used without written permission, except digital images of the front and back covers may be resized and shown as "fair use" for purposes of selling and promoting the book.

CONTENTS

George Washington. 9
- Masonic Life During the American Revolution
- Formation of the Grand Lodges in America
- Washington as Grand Master
- Temple of Virtue & Society of Cincinnati
- Masonic Apron of Washington
- Presidential Election & Masonic Oath at Inauguration
- Laying of the *Southeast* Cornerstone of U.S. Capitol & Masonic Ceremony
- Retirement from Public Life & Congratulations from the Grand Lodge of Boston
- The Illuminati & Fame as a Freemason
- Final Year & Masonic Burial
- Masonic Reaction After the Death of Washington
- Laying of the Cornerstone of Washington Monument
- Laying of the Cornerstone of Washington D.C.

Paul Revere 179
- Laying of the Cornerstone of Boston, Massachusetts State House

- The Golden Urn Fashioned by Paul Revere

Benjamin Franklin 193
- The Society of the Free and Easy
- Printing of the First American Constitution of Freemasonry
- Burning of Young Man in Farce Masonic Ceremony
- French Masonic Medal & Last Days

John Sullivan 213
- Wilderness March & Masonic Ceremonies
- The Warring Conflict of Two Masons
- Sullivan Elected Grand Master

Joseph Warren 224
- Masonic Monument to General Warren
- Bunker Hill Monument

Index 237

List of References Consulted . . . 239

Illustrations

George Washington	9
Emblem of American Union Lodge	13
Washington Lodge.	23
Washington Masonic Medal	40
Arms of Freemasons	40
Mount Vernon	48
Jewel Made for George Washington as the First Grand Master	50
Elkanah Watson	52
Masonic Apron of George Washington	73
Bible on Which Washington Took Oath Of Office	76
Masonic Procession at Laying of Capitol Cornerstone	87
Ancient Jewel of the Grand Lodge of Maryland	90
Masonic Funeral Ceremonies During the Late 1700s	130
Washington Monument	157
General Lafayette	169
Grand Master M. M. Parker	172
Paul Revere	179
Exchange Coffee House	180
Green Dragon Tavern	181
Sign of the Green Dragon Tavern	181
Silver Masonic Jewels Fashioned by Paul Revere	182
Boston's State Street – 1801	184
Old Boston State House	186
Golden Urn with Washington's Hair	191
Benjamin Franklin	193
Tun Tavern	196
John Sullivan, LL, D.	213

Joseph Warren	225
Samuel Adams	227
Masonic Monument in Memory of General Joseph Warren	233
Bunker Hill Monument	236

"It was some time since that a book fell into my hands, entitled 'Proofs of a Conspiracy, etc.,' by John Robison, which gives a full account of a Society of Freemasons, that distinguishes itself by the name of 'Illuminati,' whose plan is to overturn all government and all religion, even natural, and who endeavor to eradicate every idea of a Supreme Being, and distinguish man from beast by his shape only."

> G. W. Snyder to George Washington
> Aug. 22, 1798.

"It was not my intention to doubt that the doctrines of the *Illuminati*, and the principles of *Jacobinism* had not spread in the United States. On the contrary, no one is more fully satisfied of this fact than I am."

> George Washington to G. W. Snyder
> Oct. 24, 1798

George Washington
Portrait from Life by William Williams
September 1794

Masonic Life During the American Revolution

The commencement of the American Revolution was a new era in the Masonic as well as political history of our country. As the biographer of Washington's public history is obliged to trace it along the pathway of current public events, so also his Masonic life, when fully given, must be blended with the Masonic history of the times in which he lived.

From the first introduction of warranted lodges into America in 1733, until the commencement of the Revolution, Masonry had been in a state of progress in this country, so that in 1774 there were warranted lodges in each of the thirteen colonies, and in seven of them Provincial Grand Lodges. Massachusetts and Pennsylvania had then each two grand bodies of this class, making nine supervising Masonic powers in the colonies; and when we add to these the Grand Lodges of Scotland, Ireland, and the two of England, which each exercised Masonic authority in this country, we find the sources of Masonic power in the colonies then to be thirteen. The number of their subordinate lodges is lost to history, and the roll of the workmen who wrought upon the first temple of American Masonry has passed into the archives of the Grand Lodge above. The foundations of that temple still remain, but

"Its walls are dust, its trowels rust
Its builders with the saints, we trust."

In 1774, when the clouds of political adversity were gathering thick above our country, and seemed ready to burst upon it with all their complicated gloom, a congress of delegates from the different colonies was convened at Philadelphia, and Washington was a member from Virginia. There were assembled in that council-chamber men who had never met before.

From New England, from the banks of the Hudson, the Delaware, the Susquehanna, and the Potomac, and from far down in the sunny South they came, and all looked kindly on each other then; for Common dangers and a common weakness bespoke the necessity of a unity of action. Many brothers of the mystic tie were members of that body, and over its deliberations Peyton Randolph, the Provincial Grand Master of Virginia, was selected from the bright roll of master workmen, to preside. Mr. Adams said it was a collection of the greatest men upon this continent, in point of abilities, virtues, and fortunes. Washington's position in it may be seen from a remark made by Patrick Henry, who was also a member, to one who asked him whom he considered the greatest man in that body. "If you speak of eloquence," said he, "Mr. Rutledge of South Carolina is by far the greatest orator; but if you speak of solid information and sound judgment, Colonel Washington is unquestionably the greatest man on that floor."

A second session of which Washington was also a member, assembled the following year in Philadelphia, and Mr. Randolph was again called to preside over its councils. His health, however, failing, John Hancock was elected his successor as president; and before the session closed. Mr. Randolph died, and his remains were taken to Virginia and buried with Masonic honors. The contest at arms between the colonies and the mother country had already begun at Concord and Lexington, and Washington was elected commander-in-chief of the American army. He was at this time forty-three years of age. He had left his home at Mount Vernon but a few weeks before, expecting soon to return; but the duties of his appointment admitted of no delay, and after giving a few written directions for his domestic business, and executing a will, which he inclosed in an affectionate letter to his wife, who repaired to Cambridge, where the army was then stationed.

The British troops then held possession of Boston; and the very day that Washington received his commission, the battle of Bunker Hill was fought, and hi it fell General Joseph Warren, Grand Master of the Massachusetts Grand Lodge. It was the first grand offering of American Masonry at the altar of liberty, and the ground floor of her temple was bloodstained at its eastern gate. The second Grand Master who fell at the post of duty, was Peyton Randolph, in the following October, whose death has been already noticed. One fell on the battlefield, and the other in the council chamber of our country. Both their graves were wet with a nation's tears, and their Masonic brethren placed on each the green acacia.

Washington reached Cambridge on the 2nd of July, and on the following day took command of the army. There were gathered around him a stern band of determined men, who had left their peaceful avocations and taken arms to defend their hearthstones. Of uniform they had little, and their arms were such as were found in possession of men unused to war. Some of their officers had -before held command in the old French and Indian War, and some had never held a sword before. To maintain his numbers, provide for their necessities, and reduce them to discipline, was Washington's first care. But the year closed dark and gloomy upon the prospects of the army. Mrs. Washington left Mount Vernon late in the fall to spend the winter months at headquarters, and many of the officers were also joined by their wives; but the other officers and soldiers had few pleasures in their winter-quarters to make them forget the homes they had left.

During the previous French and Indian War, military lodge warrants had been granted by the Grand Lodge of Massachusetts to brethren in the army; and at the close of wearisome marches, and in their cheerless camps, the Masonic lodge-room became a bivouac in the tired soldier's life, where his toils and privations were forgotten, and the finest feelings of his heart cultivated. While the Connecticut line of the army was encamped during this winter at Roxbury, near Boston, a movement was made by the brethren in it, early in February, to establish a Masonic lodge in their camp. For this purpose they applied to the Grand Officers of the Grand Lodge of Massachusetts, of which John Howe was Grand Master, and Colonel Richard Gridley his Deputy, for the necessary authority. The petition was signed by Colonel Samuel H. Parsons, Colonel Samuel Wyllys, Colonel Joel Clark, Major John Park, Major Thomas Chase, Captain Ezekiel Scott, and sundry other brethren, praying that they might be formed into a regular lodge.

By appointment from Colonel Richard Gridley, the Deputy Grand Master, a meeting of the brethren was held in the Roxbury camp, on the 13th of February, 1776. At this meeting, it was agreed that Colonel Clark be recommended as Master, Major Park as Senior Warden, Major Chase as Junior Warden, Colonel Parsons as Treasurer, and Ensign Jonathan Hart as Secretary. The foregoing proceedings having been presented to the Deputy Grand Master, who was not present at the meeting, upon the 15th of the same month he issued to them a warrant or dispensation to hold a lodge in their camp at Roxbury, or wherever their body should remove on the continent of America, provided it was where no other Grand Master held authority.

It was called American Union Lodge, and both its name and the device on its seal were significant of the aid lent by Masonry in the hour of our country's need. Both were expressive of the great sentiment which then pervaded the American heart. If Liberty was its keynote, Union was its watchword. The union of the Anglo-American colonies for mutual defence had been proposed in 1741, by Daniel Coxe of New Jersey, the first Provincial Grand Master in America. It had again been advocated in 1754 by Dr. Franklin, Provincial

Grand Master of Pennsylvania, who also symbolized the idea at the close of an essay, which he published on this subject, by a wood-cut representing a snake divided into parts, with the initial letter of each colony on a separate part, underneath which he placed the motto, "Join or Die."

The purposes for which both Coxe and Franklin had unsuccessfully advocated a federal union of the colonies, had been to protect them against the French "When the Revolution commenced, and the union of the colonies against British aggression was urged, many of the newspapers adopted Franklin's device and motto. When the Union had taken place, the device was changed as a newspaper heading, and a coiled rattlesnake, with its head erect to strike, was substituted, with the motto, "Don't tread on me." Both these devices and mottoes were inscribed on flags and other ensigns of war of the provincial troops at the commencement of the Revolution. This device, as a colonial emblem, was soon after changed to a circle consisting of a chain with thirteen links, containing in each an initial letter of one of the thirteen colonies. It was also placed upon some of the currency of the colonies as early as 1776.

The seal of American Union Lodge bore the same popular American idea in its symbolism, having as its principal device a chain of thirteen circular links, around a central part, on which was the square and compasses, with the sun, moon, and a star above, and three burning tapers beneath them, the extremities of the chain being united by two clasped hands. For the leading idea of the symbolism of the chain representing the union of the colonies, the brethren were probably indebted to Dr. Franklin, who visited the American camp in 1770, as one of a committee from Congress to confer with Washington on the affairs of the war; and the seal is supposed to have been engraved by Paul Revere, a distinguished Mason and patriot of Massachusetts, who was often employed at that period to engrave such designs.

Although a Military Lodge warrant had been granted by the Masonic authorities of New York on the 24th of July, 1775, for a lodge in the provincial troops of that colony, which was called St. John's Regimental Lodge, yet the American Union Lodge was the first organized in the *Continental* army, and may be justly regarded as the eldest Masonic daughter of the American Union. It was organized in troops of which Washington had command, and though his military duties did not admit of his attendance on its meetings during the time the army was encamped around Boston, he subsequently often joined his Masonic brethren within its walls, and ever inculcated among its members, both by precept and example, a love of Masonry. This lodge went with his army, when it removed to New York, and held its meetings there while the city remained in his possession. Its last meeting there was on the 15th of August, 1776, a few days before the disastrous battle on Long Island. The next subsequent record of this lodge states:

"The British troops having landed with a large body on Long Island, the attention of the American army was necessary to repel them. On the ever memorable 27th of August, the Right Worshipful Joel Clark, Elisha Hopkins, Ozias Bissell, Joseph Jewett, Nathaniel Gore, being taken prisoners; and on the 13th of September, Brother James Chapman, Micajah Gleason, killed; William Cleavland and John P. Wyllys taken prisoners, and Brother Otho H. Williams taken prisoner at Fort Washington, by which misfortunes the lodge was deprived of its Master, and some most worthy members, and many other brethren were called to act in separate departments, wherefore the lodge stood closed without day.

"(Signed) Jonathan Hart, Secretary."

No further meetings of this lodge were held until March, 1777; and in the mean time, Joel Clark, its Master, died in captivity.

After the disastrous battle of Long Island, Washington found it impossible for the safety of his army to retain possession of New York, and he evacuated the city about the middle of September, after having his headquarters there five months. From this time until the close of 1776, he did not long enjoy a resting-place for his troops. His strongholds upon the Hudson were lost, and he retreated from river to river in New Jersey, till he had crossed the Delaware, and encamped on its Pennsylvania side. There he turned upon his pursuers, and on the 25th of December re-crossed the river amidst floods of ice, surprised a portion of the British army while engaged in their Christmas revels at Trenton, and gained a decided victory. This at once turned the tide of war, and after further successes at Princeton, his army went into winter-quarters at Morristown.

The close of 1776 was the darkest period in the history of American Masonry. Every Grand East on the American continent was shrouded in darkness. Massachusetts and Virginia had each lost a Grand Master since the commencement of the war; the old Grand Lodge of New York was dissolved, by its Grand Master, Sir John Johnson, fleeing from his home, and becoming an officer in the British army; the labors of the Grand Lodge of Pennsylvania were suspended, and their hall was soon after made a prison-room for citizens who were disaffected to the American cause.

In the spring of 1777 a ray of light first arose in the East. The members remaining of Dr. Warren's Grand Lodge were convened, and they resolved, that as the political head of this country had destroyed all connection between the States and the country from which that Grand Lodge derived its commissioned authority, it was their privilege to assume an elective supremacy, and they accordingly elected Joseph Webb their Grand Master. Virginia, too, a few months later, called a convention of its lodges, which recommended to its constituents George Washington as the most proper person to be elected the first independent Grand Master of Virginia. Washington at that time had held no official position in Masonry, and he modestly declined the intended honor, when informed of the wish of his Virginia brethren, for two reasons: first, he did not consider it masonically legal, that one who had never been installed as Master or Warden of a lodge, should be elected Grand Master; and second, his country claimed at the time all his services in the tented field. John Blair, therefore, the Master of Williamsburg Lodge, who was an eminent citizen of Virginia, was elected in his stead.

The military campaign of 1777 gave to history, in quick succession, the battles of Brandywine and Germantown, the evacuation of Philadelphia by Congress, and its occupation by British troops, and closed by the retirement of the American army into winter-quarters at Valley Forge. Here, as the shoeless army marched to their cheerless encampment, hundreds of bare feet left footprints of blood in their frozen path. Washington was moved to tears at the sight, and his touching exclamation of *"poor fellows"* was responded to by a "God bless your Excellency, your poor soldiers' friend," by the suffering soldiers. Masonic traditions state that military lodges were held in the camp at Valley Forge, which Washington often attended, but the loss of their records prevents us from verifying the statement. His headquarters that winter were at the house of a Quaker preacher; and tradition has told us how the man of peace surprised him one day in a retired place, praying audibly and fervently for the success of the American arms, and that he thereupon assured his family that America would finally triumph, for such prayers would surely be answered.

"Oh! who shall know the might
Of the words he utter'd there?
The fate of nations then was turn'd
By the fervor of that prayer.

"Hut wouldst thou know his *words*,
Who wander'd there alone?
Go, read enroll'd in heaven's archives
The prayer of Washington!"

There is an interesting Masonic memorial of Washington at this period, which has long been in possession of Lodge No. 43, at Lancaster, Pennsylvania. While Congress held its sessions in York, during the time the British occupied Philadelphia, Washington visited that borough, and his striking and majestic appearance so impressed a young man of that vicinity, that he carved a life-size statue of him from a single block of wood, which was afterwards presented to Lodge No. 43, and is still in its possession. The name of the young self-taught artist who carved it has long been forgotten, but the outlines and expression of the statue are said to bear a striking resemblance to Washington at that period.

During the following, year the British troops evacuated Philadelphia, and the campaign of 1778 closed with the contending armies in nearly the same position as they were in the summer of 1776. In the latter part of December, Washington visited Philadelphia, where Congress was in session; and while there, the Grand Lodge of Pennsylvania celebrated the festival of St. John the Evangelist. Washington was present on the occasion, and was honored with the chief place in the procession, being supported on his right by the Grand Master, and on his left by the Deputy Grand Master. More than three hundred brethren joined in this procession. They met at nine o'clock, at the college, and being properly clothed, the officers in the jewels of their office, and other badges of their dignity, the procession moved at eleven o'clock, and proceeded to Christ Church, where a Masonic sermon, for the benefit of the poor, was preached by the Rev. Bro. William Smith, D. D., Grand Secretary of the Grand Lodge of Pennsylvania. In it he beautifully alluded to Washington, who was present, as the Cincinnatus of America; saying also, "Such, too, if we divine aright, will future ages pronounce the character of a **********; but you all anticipate me in a name, which delicacy forbids me on this occasion to mention. Honored with his presence as a Brother, you will seek to derive virtue from his example."

Great poverty and distress had been occasioned in Philadelphia by the British troops during their occupancy of the city, and in accordance with Masonic" custom, a call was made on the fraternity in this sermon for the relief of those in distress. Having eloquently presented the duty of charity, the Rev. Brother closed his discourse by saying: "But I will detain you no longer, brethren! you all pant to have a foretaste of the joy of angels, by calling into exercise this heavenly virtue of charity, whereby you will give glory to the Thrice Blessed Three, Father, Son, and Holy Ghost, one God over all!" At the word "glory," the brethren rose together; and in reverential posture, on pronouncing the names of the Triune God, accompanied the same by a corresponding repetition of the ancient sign or symbol of Divine homage and obeisance, concluding with the following response, "Amen! So let it ever be!" More than four hundred pounds were immediately collected for the relief of the poor, and the Grand Lodge of Pennsylvania was made on the occasion the almoner of Washington's bounty. This sermon of Dr. Smith was published soon after, by direction of the Grand Lodge, and the profits arising from its sale were also given to the poor. The pamphlet was prefaced with the following dedication to Washington:

"To his Excellency, George Washington, Esq., general and commander-in-chief of the armies of the United States of North America the friend of his country and mankind, ambitions of no higher title, if higher were possible the following sermon, honored with his presence when delivered, is dedicated in testimony of the sincerest brotherly affection and esteem of his merit.
"By order of the Brethren,
"John Coats,
"Grand Secretary, *pro tem*"

No earlier production, either literary or Masonic, had been dedicated to Washington. "We regret the want of Masonic records to give the names of other visiting brethren who were present at this festival. An ode commemorative of Washington's participating in the ceremonies, and the position he occupied, was written a few months after by Colonel John Park, a distinguished member of American Union Lodge, addressed to Colonel Proctor, of Pennsylvania, bearing date, February 7, 1779, in which he says:

"See Washington, he leads the train,
'Tis he commands the grateful strain;
See, every crafted son obeys,
And to the godlike brother homage pays.
*   *   *   *   *
  *   *   *

Let fame resound him through the land,
And echo, *'Tis our Master Grand!*
*   *   *   *   *
  *   *   *

'Tis he our ancient craft shall sway, -
Whilst we, with *three times three, obey.*"

We have no doubt, from this time onward it was the desire of many of the brethren, especially those in the army, to see Washington placed at the head of American Masonry. At a public festival of American Union Lodge, held at Beading, in Connecticut, on the 25th of March, 1779, the first toast given was, "General Washington;" which was followed by one to "*The memory of* Warren, Montgomery, *and* Wooster," three distinguished Masons who had fallen on the battlefields of the Revolution. From this time onward the name of Washington became a Masonic toast, and the first in order at all Masonic festivals.

On the 23d of June, Washington established his headquarters at Now "Windsor, on the Hudson, near Newburg. The following day American Union Lodge met at Nelson's Point, and proceeded from thence to West Point to celebrate the festival of St. John the Baptist. Being joined by a number of Masonic brethren from the brigades there, and on Constitution Island, they proceeded from General John Patterson's quarters, on the opposite side of the river, to the Robinson House, where they retired to a bower in front of the house, and were joined by General Washington and his family. Here addresses were delivered by Rev. Dr. Hitchcock and Major William Hull (afterwards General Hull of the war of 1812). Dinner, music, toasts, and songs closed the entertainment. Washington then returned to his barge, attended by the wardens and secretary of the lodge, amidst a crowd of brethren, the music playing "God save America;" and as he and his family embarked to recross the river to New Windsor, his departure was announced by three cheers from the shore, which were answered by three from the barge, the music beating the "Grenadiers' March."

Many distinguished officers of the army, who were Masons, were present at this festival; and the brethren in the Massachusetts line soon after petitioned the Massachusetts Grand Lodge for a warrant to hold a traveling lodge in their camp. The petition was granted on the 6th of October, 1779, constituting General John Patterson, Master, and Colonel Benjamin Tupper and Major William Hull, Wardens. The lodge was called "WASHINGTON LODGE." Captain Moses Greenleaf of the Eleventh Massachusetts Regiment afterwards became Master of this lodge. His son, Simon Greenleaf, late Past Grand Master of Maine, said he had often heard his father mention Washington's visits to this lodge while commander-in-chief, and the high gratification they gave to the officers and members, especially as he went without ceremony, as a private brother.

Washington Lodge

Formation of Grand Lodges in America
&
Washington as Grand Master

At the close of 1779, Washington's headquarters were again at Morristown, New Jersey, where they had been during the winter of 1776-77. Here the American Union Lodge was again at work, and also various other military lodges, which had been organized in the American army. On the 27th of December, the American Union Lodge met to celebrate the festival of St. John the Evangelist. Besides the regular members of the lodge present, the record shows the names of sixty-eight visiting brethren, one of whom was Washington. At a previous meeting of this lodge, held on the 15th of December, its records show that its Master, Major Jonathan Habt, was appointed one of a joint committee from the various military lodges in the army "to take into consideration some matters for the good of Masonry." At the festival meeting on the 27th, "a petition was read, representing the present state of Free-Masonry to the several Deputy Grand Masters in the United States of America, desiring them to adopt some measures for appointing a Grand Master over said States." It was ordered that this petition be circulated through the different lines of the army; and also "that a committee be appointed from the different lodges in the army, from each line, and from the staff of the army, to convene on the first Monday of February next, at Morristown, to take the foregoing petition into consideration." This committee accordingly met at Morristown, on the 7th day of

February, 1780, and the following is a copy of its proceedings:

"At a committee of Ancient Free and Accepted Masons, met this 7th day of the second month in the year of Salvation, 1780, according to the recommendation of a Convention Lodge, held at the celebration of St. John the Evangelist.

"Present, Brother John Pierce, M. M., delegated to represent the Masons in the military line of the State of Massachusetts Bay, and Washington Lodge, No. 10; Brother Jonathan Hart, M. M., delegated to represent the Masons in the military line of the State of Connecticut, and American Union Lodge; Brother Charles Graham, F. C., delegated to represent the Masons in the military line of the State of New York; Brother John Sanford, M. M., delegated to represent the Masons in the military line of the State of New Jersey; Brother George Tudor, M. M., delegated to represent the Masons in the military line of the State of Pennsylvania; Brother Otho Holland Williams, M. M., delegated to represent the Masons in the military line of the State of Delaware; Brother Mordecai Gist, P. W. M., delegated to represent the Masons in the military line of the State of Maryland; Brother Prentice Brown, M. M., delegated to represent St. John's Regimental Lodge; Brother John Lawrence, P. W. M., delegated to represent the brothers in the staff of the American army; Brother Thomas Machin, M. M., delegated to represent the Masons in the corps of artillery."

The brothers present proceeded to elect a president and secretary, whereupon Brother Mordecai Gist was unanimously chosen president, and Brother Otho Holland Williams unanimously chosen secretary of this committee.

The committee proceeded to take into consideration an address to be preferred to the Eight Worshipful Grand Masters in the respective United States, whereupon Brother Williams presented the following address:

"TO THE EIGHT WORSHIPFUL,

THE GRAND MASTERS OF THE SEVERAL LODGES IN THE RESPECTIVE UNITED STATES OF AMERICA.

UNION.   FORCE.   LOVE.

"The subscribers, Ancient Free and Accepted Masons in convention, to you, as the patrons and protectors of the craft upon this continent, prefer their humble address.

"Unhappily, the distinctions of interest, the political-views, and national disputes subsisting between Great Britain and these United States have involved us, not only in the general calamities that disturb the tranquility which used to prevail in this once happy country, but in a peculiar manner affects our society, by separating us from the Grand Mother Lodge in Europe, by disturbing our connection with each other, impeding the progress, and preventing the perfection of Masonry in America.

"We deplore the miseries of our countrymen, and particularly lament the distresses which many of our poor brethren must suffer, as well from the want of temporal relief, as for want of a source of *light* to govern their pursuits and illuminate the path of happiness. And we ardently desire to restore, if possible, that fountain of charity, from which, to the unspeakable benefit of mankind, flows benevolence and love: considering with anxiety these disputes, and the many irregularities and improprieties committed by weak or wicked brethren, which too manifestly show the present dissipated and almost abandoned condition of our lodges in general, as well as the relaxation of virtue amongst individuals.

"We think it our duty, Eight Worshipful Brothers and Seniors in the Craft, to solicit your immediate interposition to save us from the impending dangers of schisms and apostasy. To obtain security from those fatal evils, with affectionate humility, we beg leave to recommend the adopting and pursuing the most necessary measures for establishing one Grand Lodge in America, to preside over and govern all other lodges of whatsoever degree or denomination, licensed or to be licensed upon the continent; that the ancient principles and discipline of Masonry being restored, we may mutually and universally enjoy the advantages arising from frequent communion and social intercourse. To accomplish this beneficial and essential work, permit us to propose that you, the Eight Worshipful Grand Masters, or a majority of your number, may nominate as Most Worshipful Grand Master of said lodge, a brother whose merit and capacity may be adequate to a station so important and elevated, and transmitting the name and nomination of such brother, together with the name of the lodge to be established, to our Grand Mother Lodge in Europe for approbation and confirmation, and that you may adopt and execute any other ways or means most eligible for preventing impositions, correcting abuses, and for establishing the general principles of Masonry, that the influence of the same in propagating morality and virtue may be far extended, and that the lives and conversation of all true Free and Accepted Masons may not only be the admiration of men on earth, but may receive the final approbation of the

Grand Architect of the Universe, in the world wherein the elect enjoy eternal light and love.

"Signed in convention, at Morristown, Morris County, this 7th day of the second month, in the year of our Saviour 1780, Anno Mundi, 5780. Which being read, was unanimously agreed to sign, and ordered to be forwarded with an extra copy of their proceedings, signed by the president and secretary, to the respective Provincial Grand Masters; and the committee adjourned without day."

There were Grand Lodges in active existence in but three of the States at this time viz., Massachusetts, Pennsylvania, and Virginia; and although the name of Washington for General Grand Master does not appear in the foregoing petition from the Masonic convention in the army, yet it was formally signified to these Grand Lodges that he was their choice. The events of the period we are now sketching are of great interest, not only in the Masonic history of Washington, but also in the Masonic history of our country. Our records show that the action of the brethren in the army was the prelude to the great changes that were soon wrought in the polity of American Masonry, and that he was first in the hearts of Masons, as well as first in the hearts of his countrymen. Previous to the reception of the address of the Army Convention by the Grand Lodge of Pennsylvania, but while these proceedings were in progress, an emergent meeting of that grand body was convened at Philadelphia, on the 13th of January, 1780, to consider the propriety of appointing a General Grand Master over all the Grand Lodges formed or to be formed in the United States; and its records show, that,

"The ballot was put upon the question whether it be for the benefit of Masonry, that a GRAND MASTER OF MASONS throughout the United States shall now be nominated on the part of this Grand Lodge; and it was unanimously determined in the affirmative.

"Sundry respectable brethren being put in nomination, it was moved that the ballot be put for them separately, and his Excellency, George Washington, Esq., general and commander-in-chief of the army of the United States, being first in nomination, he was balloted for as Grand Master, and elected by the unanimous vote of the whole lodge.

"Ordered, that the minutes of this election and appointment be transmitted to the different Grand Lodges in the United States, and their concurrence therein be requested, in order that application be made to his excellency in due form, praying that he will do the brethren and Craft the honor of accepting their appointment."

A committee was chosen to expedite the business, and to inform themselves of the number of Grand Lodges in America, and the names of their officers, and prepare a circular letter to be sent them. So little was known, at this time, by the Provincial Grand Lodges in this country of their sister Grand Bodies in other States, that months elapsed before the necessary information came before the Grand Lodge of Pennsylvania, on which to act in carrying out the resolution of January 13th, relative to a correspondence in relation to the appointment of a General Grand Master. On the 27th of the following July, having learned that there was a Grand Lodge in Virginia, of which John Blair was Grand Master, the Grand Secretary was directed to write to Mr. Blair and request the concurrence of that Grand Lodge (if Ancient Masons) in the appointment of General

Washington as Grand M. General of Masons in America. A similar letter was also directed to be written to Colonel William Malcom, of Fishkill, New York; and as they had learned that there was a Grand Lodge at work in Boston, of which Colonel William Palfrey was a member, Colonel Proctor, of Philadelphia, was directed to confer with him. Having made these preliminary inquiries, the Grand Secretary of the Grand Lodge of Pennsylvania addressed the following letter to Joseph Webb, Grand Master of the Massachusetts Grand Lodge:

"Philadelphia, August 19, 1780.
"Joseph Webb, Esq.:
"Sir—I do myself the honor to address you, by orders from the Grand Lodge of Ancient York Masons, regularly constituted in the city of Philadelphia. This Grand Lodge has under its jurisdiction, in Pennsylvania and the States adjacent, thirty-one different regular lodges, containing in the whole more than one thousand brethren. Inclosed, you have a printed abstract of some of our late proceedings; and by that of January 13th last, you will observe that we have, so far as depends on us, done that honor which we think due to our illustrious brother, General Washington viz., electing him Grand Master over all the Grand Lodges formed, or to be formed, in these United States; not doubting of the concurrence of all the Grand Lodges in America to make this election effectual.

"We have been informed by Colonel Palfrey that there is a Grand Lodge of Ancient York Masons in the State of Massachusetts, and that you are Grand Master thereof. As such, I am, therefore, to request that you will lay our proceedings before your Grand Lodge, and request their concurrent voice in the appointment of General Washington, as set forth in the minutes of January 13th, which, as far as we have been able to learn, is a measure highly approved by all the brethren, and that will do honor to the Craft.

"William Smith,
"*Grand Secretary.*"

To this, Mr. Webb returned the following answer:

"Boston, September 4, 1780.

"Sir—Your agreeable favor of the 19th ult. I duly received on the 31st, covering a printed abstract of the proceedings of your Grand Lodge. I had received one near three months before, from the Master of a traveling lodge of the Connecticut line; but the evening after I received yours, it being Grand Lodge, I laid it before them, and had some debate on it. Whereupon it was agreed to adjourn the lodge for three weeks, to the 22d inst.: likewise, to write to all the lodges in this jurisdiction to attend themselves, if convenient, by their Masters and Wardens; and if not, to give instruction to their proxies here concerning their acquiescence in the proposal.

"I am well assured that no one can have any objection to so illustrious a person as General Washington to preside as Grand Master of the United States; but at the same time it will be necessary to know from you his prerogatives as such; whether he is to appoint Sub-Grand or Provincial Grand Masters of each State. If so, I am confident that the Grand Lodge of this State will never give up their right of electing their own Grand Masters and other officers annually. This induces me to write to you now, before the result of the Grand Lodge takes place; and I must beg an answer by the first opportunity, that I may be enabled to lay the same before them. I have not heard of any States, except this and yours, that have proceeded as yet, since the independence, to elect their officers, but

I have been hoping they would. I do not remember of more Grand Masters being appointed when we were under the British government, than in South Carolina, North Carolina, Pennsylvania, New York, and Massachusetts; but now it may be necessary.

"I have granted a dispensation to New Hampshire, till they shall appoint a Grand Master of their own, which I suppose will not be very soon, as there is but one lodge in that State. Inclosed, I send you a list of the officers of our Grand Lodge, and have the honor to be,

"With great respect and esteem,
"Your affectionate brother and
"Humble servant,
"Jos. Webb, G. M."

This communication was laid before the Grand Lodge of Pennsylvania, at a special Grand Communication, on the 16th of October; and a committee, consisting of Colonel Palfrey and the Grand Secretary, Dr. William Smith, was appointed to prepare an answer; and they laid the same before the Grand Body on the following evening, to which it adjourned. The following is a copy:

"Philadelphia, October 17, 1780.
"Joseph Webb, Esq.:
"RESPECTED SIR, AND RIGHT WORSHIPFUL BROTHER—Your kind and interesting letters of the 4th and 19th ult., by some delay in the Post-Office, came both to my hands together, and that not before the 10th inst. They were both read and maturely considered at a very full Grand* Lodge last evening; and I have it in charge to thank you, and all the worthy members of the Grand Lodge of Massachusetts, for the brotherly notice they were pleased to take of the proposition

communicated to you from the Grand Lodge of this State.

"We are happy to find that you agree with us in the necessity of having one complete Masonic jurisdiction under some one Grand Head throughout the United States. It has been a measure long wished for among the brethren, especially in the army; and from them the request came originally to us, that we might improve the opportunity, which our central situation gave us, of-setting the measure on foot. From these considerations, joined to an earnest desire of advancing and doing honor to Masonry, and not from any affected superiority, or of dictating to any of our brethren, we put in nomination for Grand Master over all these States (and elected so far as depended on us) one of the most illustrious of our brethren, whose character does honor to the whole Fraternity, and who, we are therefore persuaded, would be wholly unexceptionable. When our proposition and nomination should be communicated to other Grand Lodges, and ratified by their concurrence, then, and not before, it was proposed to define the powers of such a Grand Master General, and to fix articles of Masonic union among the Grand Lodges, by means of a convention of committees from the different Grand Lodges, to be held at such time and place as might be agreed upon. Such convention may also have powers to notify the Grand Master General of his election, present him with his diploma, badges of office, and install with due form and ceremony.

"To you who are so well learned in the Masonic Art, and acquainted with its history, it needs not to be observed that one Grand Master General over many Grand Lodges, having each their own Grand Master, is no novel institution: even if the peculiar circumstances of the Grand Lodges in America, now separated from the jurisdiction from whence they originated, did not render it necessary. We have also a very recent magnificent example of the same thing in Europe, which may serve, in respect to the ceremonies of installation, as a model for us. I will copy the paragraph as dated, at Stockholm, in Sweden, the 21st of March last, as you may not have seen it.

"'The 19th of this month (March, 1780) will always be a remarkable day to the Free Masons established in this Kingdom, for on that day the Duke of Sundermania was installed Grand Master of all the lodges throughout this Kingdom, as well as those in St. Petersburg, Copenhagen, Brunswick, Hamburg, etc. The lodge at St. Petersburg had sent a deputy for this purpose, and others had intrusted the diploma of installment to Baron Leganbrepud, who been last year to Copenhagen and Germany on this negotiation.

"'The installment was attended with great pomp. The assembly was composed of more than four hundred members, and was honored with the presence of the king, who was pleased to grant a charter to the lodge, taking it under his royal direction, at the same time investing the new Grand Master with an ermine cloak; after which he was placed upon a throne, clothed with the marks of his new dignity, and there received the compliments of all the members, who, according to their rank, were admitted to kiss the hand, sceptre, and cloak of the new Grand Master, and had delivered to them a silver medal, struck to perpetuate the memory of this solemnity, which passed in Exchange Hall. It is said that the king will grant revenues for the commanders, and that this Royal Lodge will receive each year an annual tribute. This solemnity hath raised the order of Free Masons from a kind of oblivion into which they were sunk.'

"What the particular authorities of the Grand Master of the United States were to be, we had not taken upon us to describe, but, as before hinted, had left them to be settled by a convention of Grand Lodges or their deputies. But this is certain, that we never intended the different Provincial or State Grand Lodges, should be deprived of the election of their own Grand Officers, or any of their just Masonic rights and authorities over the different lodges within the bounds of their jurisdiction.

"But when new lodges are to be created beyond the bounds of any legal Grand Lodge now existing,' such lodges are to have their warrants from the Grand Master General. And when such lodges become a number sufficient to be fanned into a Grand Lodge, the bounds of such Grand Lodge are to be described, and his warrants be granted by the General Grand Master aforesaid; who may also call and preside in a convention of Grand Lodges, when any matter of great or general importance to the whole United Fraternity of these United States may require it. What other powers may be given to the Grand Master General, and how such powers are to be drawn up and expressed, will be the business of the convention proposed.

"For want of some general Masonic authority over all these United States, the Grand Lodge of Pennsylvania, ex necessitate, have granted warrants beyond its bounds, to Delaware and Maryland States; and you have found it expedient to do the same, in New Hampshire: but we know that necessity alone can be the plea for this.

"By what has been said above, you will see that our idea is to have a General Grand Master over all the United States, and each lodge under him to preserve its own rights, jurisdiction, etc., as formerly under the Grand Lodge of Great Britain, from whence the Grand Lodges of America had derived their Warrants, and to have this new Masonic Constitution, and the powers of the General Grand Master, fixed by a convention aforesaid.

"Others, we are told, have proposed that there be one Grand Master over all the States, and that the other Masters of Grand Lodges, whether nominated by him, or chosen by their own Grand Lodges, should be considered as his deputies. But we have the same objection to this that you have, and never had any idea of establishing such a plan, as has been suggested before.

"This letter is now swelled to a great length. We have, therefore, only to submit two things to your deliberation: 1st. Either, whether it would be best to make your election of a General Grand Master immediately, and then propose to us a time and place where a committee from your body could meet a committee from ours to fix his powers and proceed to installment; or, 2d. Whether you will first appoint a place of meeting, and the powers of the proposed Grand Master; then return home and proceed to the election, and afterwards meet anew for installment. This last mode would seem to require too much time, and would not be so agreeable to our worthy brethren in the army, who are anxious to have this matter completed.

"As you will probably choose the first mode, could not the place of meeting be at, or near, the headquarters of the army, at, or soon after, St. John's-day next? At any rate, you will not fix a place far northward, on account of some brethren from Virginia who will attend. For we propose to advertise the business, and the time and place of meeting, in the public papers, that any regular Grand Lodges which we in ay not have heard of, may have an opportunity of sending representatives. Your answer, as soon as possible, is requested, under cover to Peter Baynter, Postmaster of Philadelphia.

"I am, etc., by order,
"William Smith, *Grand Secretary.*"

The Grand Lodge of Massachusetts having submitted the consideration of the matter to her subordinates, one of her lodges at Machias, in Maine, passed the following resolutions, as shown by this record.

"At a meeting of Warren Lodge, held at Machias, Maine, October 31, 1780, the subject of appointing a General Grand Master of all the United States was proposed, and the following resolutions were adopted:

"*First*, That it will be for the advancement of Masonry, that a Grand Master of Masons be appointed throughout the United States of America.

"*Second*, That the said Grand Master be chosen annually on the feast of St. John the Baptist, by a majority of the Grand Lodges throughout the United States of America, or at such other time as they shall judge necessary.

"*Third*, That the said Grand Master shall have no power but what shall, from time to time, be delegated to him by a majority of the Grand Lodges throughout the United States of America.

"*Fourth*, That the said Grand Master call a convention of all the Grand Lodges in the United States, within three months after his election, at such place as he shall judge most conducive to the good of the Craft; such convention to consist of one person chosen from each Grand Lodge.

"*Fifth*, That the Grand Master sit as president of the convention, to examine into any abuses that may have crept into Masonry, and rectify the same, examine the Book of Constitutions, abrogate, make, or alter laws, if they shall judge necessary, and lay their proceedings before the Grand Lodges for their approbation.

"*Sixth,* That his Excellency General George Washington be General Grand Master of Masons throughout the United States of America.

"The Right Worshipful Master and Wardens are directed to write to our representatives in the Grand Lodge, informing them of our resolutions."

The Grand Lodge of Massachusetts, however, having more fully considered the subject, thought the election of a General Grand Master of the United States, at that time, premature and inexpedient, and ordered the following resolution of their Grand Body to be sent to the Grand Lodge of Pennsylvania.

"Boston, January 9, 1781.
"As the Grand Lodge have not been acquainted with the opinions of the various Grand Lodges in the United States, respecting the choice of a Grand Master General, and the circumstances of our public affairs making it impossible we should at present obtain their sentiments upon it, therefore, voted, That no determination upon the subject could, with the propriety and justice due to the Craft at large, be made by this Grand Lodge, until a general peace shall happily take place throughout the continent.
"From the Grand Lodge records,
"Wm. Haskins, *Secretary.*"

This correspondence with the Grand Lodge of Massachusetts was the last effort made by the Grand Lodge of Pennsylvania to establish a General American Head over all the lodges in this country; and in later times, when the project has been advocated by other Grand Bodies, her voice has been invariably against it. From her action in 1780 arose, undoubtedly, the widespread appellation of the title of General Grand Master to Washington, an historical error, which has not yet been eradicated in the minds of all Masons. There is no doubt that in the minds of all his Masonic compeers, after the independence of this country was attained, he was justly regarded as the GREAT PATRON OF THE FRATERNITY IN AMERICA, which led many to believe, at the time of his death, and long after, that he had held official rank as General Grand Master.

Nor was Washington's fame as a Mason, or the belief that lie was General Grand Master, confined to this country; for, in 1786, two letters in French were addressed to him, from Cape Francois, as- "*Grand Master of America*" soliciting a lodge-warrant for brethren on that island; which letters Washington caused to be laid before the Grand Lodge of Pennsylvania, and they accordingly granted the warrant. A venerable brother in Virginia also informs us that his father, who was a Mason in Scotland, emigrated to this country soon after the close of the Revolutionary War; and that he had often heard him say, that his Masonic brethren in Scotland congratulated him, when he left, on the advantages and protection he would enjoy from Masonry in this country, as General Washington they said was Grand Master of Masons here. This illusion was also perpetuated by a Masonic medal, which was struck in 1797, having on its obverse side the bust of Washington in military dress, with its legend, "G. WASHINGTON, PRESIDENT, 1797;" and on its reverse side, the emblems of Masonry, surrounded by the inscription, "AMOR, HONOR, ET JUSTICIA," and the initials, "G. W., G. G. M."

Washington Masonic Medal, 1797

Although the Grand Lodge of Pennsylvania did not succeed in creating a General Grand Mastership, and elevating Washington to that office, as was her desire, and also that of the Military Lodges of the army, from whom the proposition first sprang, yet that Grand Body still continued to regard him as first among

Arms of the Freemasons

American Masons. At her first meeting for reorganization, after the British troops evacuated Philadelphia, she had appointed a committee, of which the Rev. Dr. WM. Smith was chairman, to prepare a new Book of Constitutions. Dr. Smith accordingly digested and abridged the English Book of Constitutions used by the Ancient York Masons; and on the 22d of November, 1781, submitted to the Grand Lodge the result of his labors, which was a Book of Constitutions, &c., which has since been known as "Smith's Ahiman Rezon."

It was approved and unanimously adopted at that meeting, and ordered to be printed, with the Masons' coat of arms as a frontispiece; and the Grand Lodge further resolved, "In case our beloved and illustrious brother General Washington permit it to be dedicated to him, that his Excellency's arms be prefixed to the dedication." At a meeting of the Grand Lodge, in December, 1782, it was further resolved that Dr. Smith's Masonic sermon and prayer, which had been delivered in presence of Washington, on the 28th of December, 1778, should also be published in the work. The book was printed in 1783, with the following dedication, but Washington's coat of arms was not inserted:

"To His Excellency George Washington, ESQ.,
"*General and Commander-in-Chief of the Armies of the United States of America*:

"In testimony, as well of his exalted services to his country, as of that noble philanthropy which distinguishes him among Masons, the following Constitutions of the t most ancient and honorable fraternity of Free and Accepted Masons, by order and in behalf of the Grand Lodge of Pennsylvania, etc., is dedicated, by his Excellency's most humble servant and faithful brother,

"William Smith, *G. Secretary.*
"*June 24,* 1782."

At a meeting of the Grand Lodge, held on the 10th of June, 1787, it was ordered that the Eight Worshipful Grand Master and Deputy Grand Master present to General Washington a, copy of this Book of Constitutions; and in an inventory of his library, made by the appraisers of his estate after his death, this book appears in the schedule.

The Military Lodges of the Revolution should not be forgotten, in a just tribute to the memory of Washington. There were ten of these instituted in the American army, in the following order, and by the following authorities:

1st. St. John's Eegimental Lodge, in the United States Battalion, July 24,] 775, by the old Provincial Grand Lodge of New York (Moderns).

2d. American Union Lodge, in the Connecticut line, February 15, 1776, by the Grand Lodge of Massachusetts (Moderns).

3d. No. 19, on the Pennsylvania Grand Lodge Registry, in the first regiment of Pennsylvania artillery, May 18, 1779, by the Grand Lodge of Pennsylvania (Ancients).

4th. Washington Lodge, in the Massachusetts line, October 6, 1779, by the Massachusetts Grand Lodge (Ancients).

5th. No. 20, on the Pennsylvania Grand Lodge Registry, in a North Carolina regiment,—1779, by the Grand Lodge of Pennsylvania (Ancients).

6th. No. 27, on the Pennsylvania Grand Lodge Registry, in the Maryland line, April 4, 1780, by the Grand Lodge of Pennsylvania (Ancients).

7th. No. 28, on the Pennsylvania Grand Lodge Registry, in the Pennsylvania line, 1780, by the Grand Lodge of Pennsylvania (Ancients).

8th. No. 29, on the Pennsylvania Grand Lodge Registry, in the Pennsylvania line, July 27, 1780, by the Grand Lodge of Pennsylvania (Ancients).

9th. No. 31, on the Pennsylvania Grand Lodge Registry, in the New Jersey line, March 26, 1781, by the Grand Lodge of Pennsylvania (Ancients).

10th. No. 36, on the Pennsylvania Grand Lodge Registry, in the New Jersey line, September 2, 1782, by the Grand Lodge of Pennsylvania (Ancients).

Masonic records, and the concurrent testimony of Washington's compeers, both show that while commander-in-chief of the American revolutionary army he countenanced the establishment and encouraged the labors of these Military Lodges, wisely considering them as schools of urbanity, well calculated to disseminate those mild virtues of the heart, so ornamental to human character, and particularly useful to correct the ferocity of soldiers, and alleviate the miseries of war. The cares of his high office engrossed too much of his time to admit of his engaging in the duties of the chair; yet he found frequent opportunities to visit these lodges, and thought it no degradation to his dignity to stand there on a level with his brethren.

There were many Masonic Lodges also connected with the British army during this period, and on several occasions the warrant and other property of such lodges were captured by American troops, but in each case they were promptly returned. One of these lodges was No. 227, on the registry of the Grand Lodge of Ireland, which has claimed that Washington was made a Mason in it during the old French War. The *London Freemasons' Magazine* states, "during the Revolution, its lodge-chest fell into the hands of the Americans; they reported the circumstance to General Washington, who embraced the opportunity of testifying his estimation of Masonry in the most marked and gratifying manner, by directing a guard of honor, under a distinguished officer, should take charge of the chest, with many articles of value, and return them to the regiment. The surprise, the feeling of both officers and men, may be imagined, when they perceived the flag of truce that announced this elegant compliment from their noble opponent, but still more noble brother. The guard of honor, with their flutes playing a sacred march, the chest containing the constitution and implements of the craft, borne aloft, like another Ark of the Covenant, equally by Englishmen and Americans, who, lately engaged in the strife of war, now marched through the enfiladed ranks of the gallant regiment, that with presented arms and colors hailed the glorious act by cheers, which the sentiment rendered sacred as the hallelujahs of an angel's song."

On another occasion, "during the war of the Revolution, while the army was encamped in New Jersey, a party of American troops was sent out on a foraging expedition, and on their way fell in with a number of British soldiers, who had been placed as a guard over some baggage which was being removed to a distant place. A skirmish ensued, they were taken prisoners, and with their baggage removed to the American army. On an examination of the baggage, a Templar's sash and Master's apron were found, which excited some surprise among the soldiers, and were immediately carried to the tent of the commander-in-chief. As soon as his eye fell upon them, he gave instructions that the baggage should be carefully protected from all injury, that inquiries should be made after the owner of these articles, and if found, that he be requested to repair immediately to his tent.

"He soon made his appearance. Kind words and friendly greetings attended his reception. He was treated with the utmost care while a prisoner, and was soon after sent home to England on parole, attended by all the comforts and conveniences which it was possible to bestow upon him in those times of trouble.

This person was Sergeant Kelly of the British army, who, after his arrival home, lived to a good old age, and preserved that sash and apron with the greatest care. On his dying bed, surrounded by his kindred—and among the number was an old and tried friend, who was a brother Mason—he ordered the sash and apron to be produced, and calling his old friend and brother to his side, exacted from him a promise, to forward, after his death, the same to Montgomery Lodge, in the city of New York, with an accompanying letter, stating it to be a memento to the fraternity, of the kindness and fraternal regard of George Washington towards an humble brother and a stranger; and as a testimonial that 'the memory of the just is blessed, and shall live and flourish like the green bay-tree.' These relics were presented to Montgomery Lodge in 1838, where they now remain, and are preserved with care."

A military alliance with France had been formed in 1778, by which auxiliary French troops were sent to America; and early in 1781, Washington visited Rhode Island to confer with the French commander on the approaching campaign. A lodge existed there, known as King David's Lodge, whose warrant had been granted by George Harrison, Provincial Grand Master of New York, to Moses M. Hays, a Jewish citizen of New York city, bearing date February 17, 1769, empowering him to hold a lodge in that city. This warrant he had taken to Rhode Island in 1780, and was then holding a lodge under it in Newport. Haying learned that Washington was daily expected there, this lodge, upon the 7th of February, 1781, appointed a committee, consisting of Mr. Hays and others, for the purpose of preparing an address, in behalf of the lodge, to present to him. At a meeting of the lodge, held at the request of the Master, February 14th, this committee reported, "That, on inquiry, they find General Washington not to be a Grand Master of North America, as was supposed, nor even Master of any particular lodge; they are therefore of opinion, that this lodge would not choose to address him as a private brother, and at the same time they think it would not be agreeable to our worthy brother to be addressed as such." The lodge therefore voted that the address be entirely laid aside for the present.

The campaign of this year is ever memorable for the capture of Cornwallis at Yorktown. "In that village," says the Honorable Robert G. Scott, of Virginia, "was Lodge No. 9, where, after the siege had ended, Washington, La Fayette, Marshall, and Nelson came together, and by their union bore abiding testimony to the beautiful tenets of Masonry."

The surrender of Cornwallis was a day of jubilee in the American army, and Washington ordered all offenders in the camp who were under arrest, to be pardoned and set at liberty. He also acknowledged an overruling Providence in their success, by directing that divine services should be held in the army, and public acknowledgments rendered to God for his signal interposition in their behalf. But it was not the army alone that gave way to joy and thanksgiving on this occasion, for the whole country was jubilant. "The news of the surrender," says a writer of that day, "reached Philadelphia between one and two o'clock at night. The watchman in those days were in the habit of calling the hour. They were all Germans, and the welkin resounded *'Oh, bast two o'clock; und* Cornwallis *is taken!'* Windows were thrown up by ladies in night-caps to catch the sound, and forthwith every house was illuminated." Congress also appointed a day of national thanksgiving, and voted thanks and other testimonials to Washington and his officers.

But while the heart of America beat wildly with joy on this occasion, that of Washington was smitten with grief by a deep domestic affliction; for he was compelled to hasten from the field of his recent triumph to Eltham, a few miles distant, to attend the deathbed of his stepson, John Parke Custis, the only remaining one of the two children of his wife at the time of his marriage. Washington, who had never had children or his own, had loved these with all a parent's fondness. The daughter had died just before the war, and his grief on that occasion was equaled only by that of Mrs. Washington. She had then just grown to womanhood, and was called *the dark-eyed lady of Mount Vernon.*

The loss of John Parke Custis, who had served as one of his aid-de-camps during a part of the war, and who had contracted his death-fever at Yorktown, was keenly felt by Washington, and he at once adopted his two youngest children as his own, and they became *the children of Mount Vernon* of after-years. These, too, were a boy and girl, whose names as "George Washington Parke Custis" and "Nelly Custis," were long interwoven with the associations of Mount Vernon.

Mount Vernon

We may be permitted to give one other scene in Washington's domestic relations at this time, and carry the reader with us to the home of his mother at Fredericksburg, which he visited soon after the battle of Yorktown. No pageantry of war, no sounding trumpets, no waving banners announced his coming. She was alone, and her aged hands were diligently employed in domestic industry, as Washington approached her threshold. A smile of recognition, a warm embrace, and the endearing name of George, uttered with trembling lips, were a mother's greeting. As she inquired concerning his health, she marked the lines of care and toil that seven years had traced on his manly brow, and then spoke of old friends and associations, but of his present fame and glory not a word. Washington had been accompanied to Fredericksburg by many distinguished officers of the French and American armies, and the citizens of Virginia for many miles around gathered there to welcome the conquerors of Cornwallis. In the evening a splendid entertainment was provided, to which the mother of Washington was specially invited. She remarked that her dancing days were past, but that she should feel happy in contributing to the festivities of the occasion, and consented to attend. When the elegant circle, composed of French and American chivalry, graced with the beauty of the smiling daughters of Virginia, was formed, Washington entered the room with his mother leaning on his arm, dressed in the plain but becoming garb of the Virginia lady of the olden time. To the attentions and greetings she received from the companions in arms of her son, the renowned warriors of two continents, her words were dignified and courteous, al-though her manners were reserved. No complimentary attentions that were shown to her produced haughtiness in her demeanor; and at an early hour, wishing the company much pleasure in their entertainment, she remarked it was "high time for old folks to be in bed," and retired, leaning as before on the arm of her son. Those foreign officers who had seen the pageantry and pride of the artificial distinctions of society in the Old World, looked with wonder and admiration on the Spartan plainness of the mother of Washington; and remarked, that a country which produced such mothers, might well boast of illustrious sons.

Jewel Made for George Washington as the First Grand Master

The Temple of Virtue
&
The Society of Cincinnati

At the close of the campaign of 1781, La Fayette, believing the war virtually closed, returned to France. He had enlisted in our cause during the darkest period of the Revolution, and had been an angel of hope to Washington, when despondence was written on the brow of many an American soldier. Of all the names on the bright roll of our country's history during the Revolution, that of La Fayette stands next to Washington.

La Fayette is supposed to have been made a Mason in one of the Military Lodges of this country, but the record of it is lost. Traditions which we shall consider in their proper place, state that it was at Morristown at Newburg at Albany and perhaps at other places that he received his degrees, and even that Washington presided as Master on some of those occasions. While we are unable to verify these, we entertain no doubt that the Masonic tie existed between them at this time, and was strongly felt.

Elkanah Watson

Washington was well known in France as a Mason at this period; and a Franco-American mercantile firm there, composed of Messrs. Watson & Cassoul, both of whom were Masons, wishing to send some testimony of respect to him, procured some nuns in a convent at Nantes to manufacture a Masonic sash and apron of the finest satin, wrought with gold and silver tissue, on which the French and American flags were combined with various Masonic emblems beautifully delineated. They were executed in a superior and expensive style, and forwarded from France to Washington, accompanied by the following letter. Mr. Watson had known General Washington in America. He was the youthful officer who had charge of the convoy of powder from Providence to the American camp, when they were so destitute of that article before Boston.

"To his Excellency General Washington, *America*:

"MOST ILLUSTRIOUS AND RESPECTED BROTHER—In the moment when all Europe admire and feel the effects of your glorious efforts in support of American liberty, we hasten to offer for your acceptance a small pledge of our homage Zealous lovers of liberty and its institutions, we have experienced the most refined joy in seeing our chief and brother stand forth in its defence, and in defence of a new-born nation of republicans.

"Your glorious career will not be confined to the protection of American liberty, but its ultimate effect will extend to the whole human family, since Providence has evidently selected you as an instrument in His hands to fulfill His eternal decrees.

"It is to you, therefore, the glorious orb of America, we presume to offer Masonic ornaments as an emblem of your virtues. May the Grand Architect of the universe be the guardian of your precious days, for the glory of the western hemisphere and the entire universe. Such are the vows of those who have the favor to be, by all the known numbers,

"Your affectionate brothers,

"Watson & Cassoul.
"East of Nantes, 23d 1st month, 5782."

Washington replied to this letter as follows, from his headquarters at Newburg:

"State of New York, August 10, 1782.
"Gentlemen—The Masonic ornaments which accompanied your brotherly address of the 23d of January last, though elegant in themselves, were rendered more valuable by tho flattering sentiments and affectionate manner in which they were presented.

"If my endeavors to avert the evil with which the country was threatened by a deliberate plan of tyranny, should be crowned with the success that is wished, the praise is due to the GRAND ARCHITECT of the universe, who did not see fit to suffer His superstructure of justice to be subjected to the ambition of the princes of this world, or to the rod of oppression in the hands of any power upon earth.

"For your affectionate vows, permit me to be grateful, and offer mine for true brothers in all parts of the world, and to assure you of the sincerity with which I am,

                    "Yours,
                    "G°. Washington.
"Messrs. Watson & Cassoul, East of Nantes."

This letter is still in the hands of the family of Mr. Watson, at Port Kent, New York. It is the earliest Masonic correspondence of Washington that is known to be extant. The sash and apron to which it relates were often worn by Washington, and were after his death presented by his legatees to Washington Lodge, No. 22, at Alexandria, where they are still preserved.

Our sketch now leads us again to the banks of the Hudson, near Newburg, where the principal northern forces under Washington were stationed. Here, in 1782-3, in rude huts erected to shelter them, they awaited the progress of events which might close their military labors, and secure to them the boon for which they had endured years of toil, privations, and peril; or which might require them to again renew their weary marches, and bare their breasts in deadly conflicts.

Many Military Lodges existed in the army at this period, but the records of most of them are lost. So well established had these camp-lodges become, and so beneficial to the brethren, that in providing the necessary conveniences for the troops in their quarters on the Hudson at this time, an Assembly-room, or Hall was built, one of the purposes of which was to serve as a Lodge-room for the Military Lodges. Washington himself ordered the erection of the building. It was a rude wooden structure, forming an oblong square, forty by sixty feet, was one story in height, and had but a single door. Its windows were square unglazed openings, elevated so high as to prevent the prying gaze of the cowan. Its timbers were hewed, squared, and numbered for their places; and when the building was finished, it was joyously dedicated, and called *"The Temple of Virtue."*

This *Temple*, or "Assembly-room," as it was sometimes called, was not appropriated exclusively to Masonic purposes; but on the Sabbath it was used as a chapel for religious services, and at other times for meetings of the officers of the army, and also for dancing and other festive amusements. The American Union Lodge met in this room on the 24th of June, 1782, preparatory to celebrating the festival of St. John the Baptist, and proceeded from thence to West Point, where they were joined by "Washington Lodge, when a procession was formed at the house of General Patterson, its first master; and both lodges proceeded from thence to the "Colonnade," where a dinner was provided, and an oration delivered by Colonel John Brooks, Master of Washington Lodge, and afterwards governor of Massachusetts. American Union Lodge then returned to their room at the temple, and closed in good time. We have no record of Washington's being present on this occasion; but at a celebration of the festival of St. John the Evangelist, on the 27th of December of the same year by King Solomon's Lodge at Poughkeepsie, Washington was present as a visitor. The imperfect records of that lodge state, that "after dinner the following address was presented to his excellency, Brother Washington:"

"We, the Master, and Wardens, and Brethren of Solomon's Lodge, No. 1, are highly sensible of the honor done to Masonry in general by the countenance shown to it by the most dignified character—."

We have given the language of this address as it stands recorded on the minute-book of the lodge; but it has the appearance of being the commencement of an address to Washington which the secretary neglected fully to record. We regret that he did not give us the full address, and Washington's reply. It was the first instance we have met with of a formal Masonic address by any lodge to Washington.

The drama of the Revolution had been virtually closed at Yorktown, in October, 1781, by the capture of Cornwallis, and the operations of the armies in the two succeeding years partook more of the nature of an armistice than of military campaigns. The principal British force remaining in America was still in possession of the city of New York, and Washington's headquarters were still at Newburg. The scenes which occurred at Newburg during the cantonment of the troops there from the autumn of 1781 to the final disbanding of the army in November, 1783, are not without interest in the Masonic history of Washington.

It was during this transition period from war to peace, when inaction had given the officers and soldiers of the army time to reflect on their past and present sufferings, and the future that was before them, that a spirit of discontent arose almost to mutiny and rebellion. Earnest but respectful solicitations had been made to Congress for relief from their embarrassments, by an adjustment of their meritorious claims; but the tardy action of that body so increased the discontent of the army, that a call was made, from a then unknown source, for a grand convention of the officers to meet and demand of Congress in unequivocal terms immediate redress. Two anonymous letters, artfully written, appealing to the passions of the army, and denouncing as a traitor to its interests any one who should venture to recommend moderation and delay, were at the same time put in circulation.

Washington saw that a crisis had come when the integrity of the army and the authority of Congress must be maintained, or all the toil, privation, and blood of the past eight years, and all the glorious hopes of the future, would be at once lost. He therefore ordered a council of his tried and trusty officers to meet at the lodge-room in the "Temple," and by his own wise counsels in it, obtained another proof of the devotion of the army, and the attachment of the officers to him as their commander.

No historian can ever determine the influence of that mystic tie that bound so many of the officers of that suffering patriot army in bonds of Masonic brotherhood to "Washington, in the happy termination of this incipient treason. He had often joined with them in the same room in Masonic labors; and while, by the constitutions of Masonry, neither the civil or military concerns of the country could have been discussed in the lodge, yet who will say that the lessons taught and learned there were not instrumental, in the hands of Washington, in directing and controlling the minds of his associate officers at this critical period. But the veil which then covered the hand that so cunningly penned those anonymous letters, which sought to draw even Washington himself from his devotion to the civil authorities, still rests on the strength of that mystic tie that bound so many of that patriot band to him, and through him to our country.

We have already noted in our sketch the strong desire of the Masonic brethren in the army that Washington should be constituted the head of Masons in this country. But as the time for the disbanding of the army drew near, and no definite action of the whole Fraternity in America had been taken, an affectionate regard of the officers for their commander, and for each other, led them to form an association among themselves, having the social features of the Masonic institution as its leading principle, and designed, by inculcating benevolence and mutual relief, to perpetuate their friendships, and incite in their minds the most exalted patriotism. The idea of such a society is said to have originated with General Knox, who communicated his plan to Baron Steuben; and at a general meeting of the officers, on the 13th of May, 1783, with the approbation of Washington, they instituted the "Society of the Cincinnati," and he became its first president, and continued to hold the office until his death.

In a sermon delivered on the 4th of July, 1790, before the State Society of the Cincinnati of Pennsylvania, by the Rev. William Smith, D. D., and provost of the college at Philadelphia, he claims that the *name* of Cincinnati for this society was adopted from a suggestion of his, in a Masonic sermon preached before the Grand Lodge of Pennsylvania in presence of Washington, on the festival of the Evangelist in 1778, in which he alludes to him as the "Cincinnatus of the age."

The newspapers of that period give an account of an earlier proposed association, or "New Order of American Knighthood," as it was called. As early as March 25, 1783, the Philadelphia papers stated that,

"On the next anniversary of Independence, the 4th of July, a new Order of Knighthood, called the Order of

Freedom, will be established, and the installation take place in the city of Philadelphia.

"Patron of the Order; St. Louis.

"Chief of the Order; President of Congress for the time being.

"Grand Master; General Washington.

"Chancellor; Dr. Franklin.

"Prelate; Dr. WITHERSPOON.

"Genealogist; Mr. Payne.

"Gentleman Usher; Mr. THOMPSON.

"Register and Secretary; Mr. DIGGS.

"Herald; Mr. HUTCHINGS.

"Twenty-four knight companions, consisting of the governor of each State for the time being, which they reckon nineteen.

"General Lincoln;—General Greene;—General Wayne;—Colonel Lee.

"The robe is to be scarlet and blue, with ermine,— the ribbon a broad satin, with thirteen alternate stripes of red and white; to which will be suspended an embossed medal of gold and enamel, on the front of which will be represented Virtue, the genius of the United States, dressed like an Amazon, resting on a spear with one hand, and holding a sword with the other, and treading on Tyranny, represented by a man prostrate, a crown fallen from his head, a broken chain in his left hand, and a scourge in his right; in the exergue, *Sic semper tyrannis*. On the reverse is a group: Liberty with her wand and Pileus; on one side of her, Ceres with a cornucopia in one hand, and an ear of wheat in the other; on the other side, Eternity, with the globe and Phoenix.

In the exergue, *Deus nobis hoc otia fecit*. The loop of the medal is to be formed by the figure of a rattlesnake with the tail in its mouth, as an emblem of eternity. An erect staff of liberty, terminated by a cap at top, will be fixed to the body of the snake, and under it the motto of *In recto decus.*"

This we believe to have been the earliest attempt in the United States to form a social institution modeled after civic distinctions of society in Europe. Who its projectors were, who its advocates, and who its opposers, we have not learned. Although such a society never went into existence, yet as it contemplated for General Washington the distinguished honor of being its Grand Master, and as a curious prelude to the formation of the Society of the Cincinnati, we have given it a place in this sketch.

The Society of the Cincinnati was designed as an association of the officers of the army after its disbanding, and of their eldest male descendants, to whom the privilege of membership was to be hereditary. It provided for a golden medal or "Order," as a badge of distinction to its members, and made provision also for funds from the attainment of membership and voluntary contribution, for the relief of its indigent members.

The Society of the Cincinnati thus became an organized body, without any known opposition either in the army or from citizens in civil life. Its associations were pleasing to its members, and they doubtless looked forward to its future meetings as social reunions, without any idea of personal aggrandizement to themselves. But a strong feeling of jealousy and opposition to the society soon sprang up in different States; and; as it was claimed by many that it created a new order of hereditary nobility, the public mind became strongly opposed to it in many of them. Pennsylvania, Massachusetts, and Connecticut officially declared the institution unjustifiable, and Rhode Island proceeded so far as to annul the civil privileges of all her citizens who -should be members of it, and declare them incapable of holding any office under her government. "While this opposition to the society in America arose from a belief that it was dangerous to the liberties of the country, it is a curious commentary on the fallibility of opinions, and the strength of prejudice, that Gustavus the Third, king of Sweden, forbade the Swedish officers who had served in the French army during the American war, to wear the badges of the Cincinnati, on the ground that the institution had a *republican* tendency, and was not suited to his government.

Washington saw, that though the institution was innocent in itself and laudable in its real objects, yet, that the prejudices of the people were too deeply disturbed by it; and by his recommendation its constitution was changed at its next annual meeting, by withdrawing all claims of its members to hereditary distinctions, disclaiming all interference with political subjects, and placing their funds under the immediate cognizance of State legislatures, retaining only their right to indulge their own private feelings of friendship, and the acts of benevolence which it was their intention should flow from them.

The social and benevolent features of this society were strikingly similar to the same features in Masonry, from which, doubtless, the leading idea was drawn. Many of its members were Masons, and as such, well understood the social influence of a union that embraced in its objects, not only the welfare and happiness of its members while living, but of their widows and orphans after them. From this institution, Masonry may also a few years later have drawn some of its principles of government in the higher bodies of the Ancient York Kite.

The autumnal months of 1783 were the last in the military life of Washington. His army had been disbanded at Newburg, and he had seen each corps of his remaining soldiers file by him for the last time, and pass onward to their homes. He then hastened to New York, where his final adieu was to be taken of his officers. The British troops had evacuated the city on the 25th of November; and on the 4th of December, at meridian, Washington's principal officers assembled at Fraunces' tavern, to take a final leave of their commander.

The scene was affecting beyond comparison. There were gathered there those who for eight long years had been his faithful associates in privations and dangers; who had followed him in many weary marches, and fought by his side in many an unequal battle. Many were there who had sat with him in the war-councils of the camp, and mingled with him in the mystic labors of the Masonic lodge-room. And now they were met to bid him, as their loved commander, a last farewell!

As Washington entered the room, and stood for the last time before them, he could not conceal his emotions. Filling a glass with wine, he raised it, and said: "With a heart full of love and gratitude, I now take leave of you; and most devoutly do I wish that your latter days may be as prosperous and happy as your former ones have been glorious and honorable." He tasted the wine, and, with voice trembling with emotion, said: "I cannot come to each of you, to take my leave; but shall be obliged to you, if each of you will come and take me by the hand." General Knox stood nearest to him. Washington grasped his proffered hand, and, incapable of utterance, drew him to his bosom with a tender embrace. Each officer in his turn received the same silent affectionate farewell: Every eye was filled with tears, every heart throbbed with emotion, but no tongue interrupted the tenderness of the scene. To those who had known him only as the stern commander; it was like Joseph's making himself known to his brethren; but to those who had met him as a brother in the lodge-room, it was but the renewal of the mystic grasp, and the well-remembered silent embrace they had each known before.

> "Weeping through that sad group he pass'd,
> Turned once, and gazed, and then was gone—
> It was his tenderest, and his last."

A corps of infantry received him at the door, and as he passed through their ranks, they saw his broad bosom heave with emotions to them unseen before; and the sobs of sorrow, and the tears that fell fast on their cheeks, told how well they loved him. Washington hastened on board a barge upon the Hudson that was ready to receive him, and as the dipping oar sped him from them, he raised his hat above his head, and bade all whom he left behind a silent adieu.

But there was still another link to be severed in the chain that bound him, as commander-in-chief, to our country, and he hastened to Annapolis, where Congress was then in session, to return to their hands the commission he had received from them eight years before, and lay before them a sword unstained with dishonor. He arrived at Annapolis on the 19th day of December, and immediately signified to Congress his purpose to resign into their hands his commission, and desired their pleasure as to the time and manner of its reception. That body, desirous of giving dignity to the spectacle, and honor to him who was its chief actor, appointed the following Tuesday, at meridian, to honor him with a public audience, and receive from his own hand the high commission he bore.

Upon the 23d of December, at the hour appointed, the closing scene in the drama of the Revolution took place. The chosen representatives of the States were each in their seats, and a few distinguished foreigners and Americans were admitted to their floor, while the gallery was crowded with citizens. As Washington entered, every spectator arose and stood uncovered, while the members of Congress, representing the supreme majesty of the people, remained covered in their seats. Nine years before he had been a member of that same body, as an honored delegate from Virginia, and had been elected from his seat, by their own wise choice, to receive a commission he now held in his hand to return again to them. But to whom was he to return it? As representing the sovereignty of the people, the body was indeed the same; but, alas! many familiar faces were not there. The first president of that body, Peyton Randolph, was not there. Loving hands had, years before, borne him to his last resting-place in the green fields of Virginia, and his Masonic brethren had planted the acacia over his grave.

As Washington advanced to offer his commission to General Mifflin, then president of the body, amidst a deep and solemn silence, he addressed him in words of felicitation on the happy termination of the war, commended the interests of our country to the protection of Almighty God, and closed by saying:

"Having now finished the work assigned me, I retire from the great theatre of action; and bidding an affectionate farewell to this august body, under whose orders I have so long acted, I here offer my commission, and take my leave of the employments of public life."

President Mifflin received his commission with words of gratitude and tenderness, and closed by saying:

"We join you in commending the interests of our dearest country to the protection of Almighty God, beseeching him to dispose the hearts and minds of its citizens to improve the opportunity afforded them of becoming a happy and respectable nation; and for you, we address to him our earnest prayers, that a life so beloved may be fostered with all his care; that your latter days may be as happy as they have been illustrious, and that he will finally give you that reward which this world cannot give."

The Masonic Apron of Washington

Washington proceeded to Mount Vernon immediately after resigning his commission at Annapolis, and arrived there on the following evening. It was the 24th of December, three days before the anniversary of St. John the Evangelist. A lodge of Freemasons had been formed in Alexandria, a few miles from his home, in the preceding February. It was working under a warrant from the Grand Lodge of Pennsylvania, and numbered, 39. Robert Adam was its Master, and many of Washington's old friends and neighbors, in and about Alexandria, were its members. This lodge was preparing to celebrate the coming festival of St. John the Evangelist, on the 27th; and the following letter, signed by the officers of the lodge, was addressed to General Washington:

"Alexandria, 26th December, 1783.
"Sir—Whilst all denominations of people bless the happy occasion of your Excellency's return to enjoy private and domestic felicity, permit us, sir, the members of Lodge No. 39, lately established in Alexandria, to assure your excellency, that we, as a mystical body, rejoice in having a brother so near us, whose pre-eminent benevolence has secured the happiness of millions; and that we shall esteem ourselves highly honored at all times your excellency shall be pleased to join us in the needful business.
 "We have the honor to be, in the name and behalf of No. 39, your Excellency's
 Devoid friends and brothers,
Robert Adam, M.,
E. C. Dick, S. W.,

J. Allison, J. W.,
Wm. Ramsey, Treas.
   "His Excellency General Washington."

Washington had but two days 'before returned to the quiet of his own loved homo, after years of toil and dangers in the camp and in the battle-field, and he might well have said to them:

"Now give mo rest; my years demand
A holiday, companions dear:
My days are drawing to an end,
And I would for that end prepare.

"Now give mo rest; but when ye meet,
Brothers, in that beloved spot,
My name with loving lips repeat,
And never let it be forgot."

Washington was unable to attend this festival, but he sent to the lodge the following reply:

        "Mount Vernon, 28th December, 1783.
   "Gentlemen—With a pleasing sensibility, I received your favor of the 26th; and beg leave to offer my sincere thanks for the favorable sentiments with which it abounds.
   "I shall always feel pleasure when it may be in my power to render service to Lodge No. 39, and in every act of brotherly kindness to the members of it, being with great truth,
      "Your affectionate brother
         and obedient servant,
            "G°. Washington.
"Robert Adam, Esq., Master,
   Wardens and Treasurer of Lodge No. 39."

Washington's feelings and employments on returning to private life may be best seen from his own correspondence; and from various letters of his written at that period, the following extracts are given:

"The scene is at last closed. * * * * On the eve of Christmas I entered these doors, an older man by nine years than when I left them. * * * * I am just beginning to experience that ease and freedom from public cares, which, however desirable, takes some time to realize. It was not till lately I could get the better of my usual custom of ruminating, as soon as I waked in the morning, on the business of the ensuing day; and of my surprise at finding, after revolving many things in my mind, that I was no longer a public man, nor had any thing to do with public transactions. ***** I hope to spend the remainder of my days in cultivating the affections of good men, and in the practice of the domestic virtues. ***** The life of the husbandman, of all others, is the most delightful. It is honorable, it is amusing, and with judicious management, it is profitable. ***** I have not only retired from all public employments, but I am retiring within myself, and shall be able to view the solitary walk, and tread the paths of private life with a heartfelt satisfaction. Envious of none, I am determined to be pleased with all; and this, my dear friend, being the order of my march, I will move gently down the stream of life, until I sleep with my fathers."

Such sentiments are so perfectly in accordance with the precepts of Masonry, that they are worthy of a place in Washington's Masonic history. But in his retirement to Mount Vernon he was not lost to the world, nor forgotten by his countrymen. "With Virginian hospitality, his doors were ever open, and all who had a claim on his friendship or his kindness were ever received with welcome; and he was ready, too, to respond to letters written to him from people of every condition, and upon every subject. But the anxiety of those who traveled abroad was so great to carry some testimonial from him, and of those who remained at home to possess some memorial of his kindness, that the labor of replying to the numerous letters addressed to him became a burden. To an intimate friend he wrote:

"It is not, my dear sir, the letters of my friends which give me trouble, or add aught to my perplexity. I receive them with pleasure, and pay as much attention to them as my avocations will permit. It is in reference to old matters with which I have nothing to do; applications which oftentimes cannot be complied with; inquiries, to satisfy which would employ the pen of an historian; letters of compliment, as unmeaning, perhaps, as they are troublesome, but which must be attended to; and commonplace business, which employ my pen and my time, often disagreeably. Indeed, these, with company, deprive me of exercise; and unless I can obtain relief, must be productive of disagreeable consequences. Already I begin to feel their effects.

"Heavy and painful oppressions of the head, and other disagreeable sensations often trouble me. I am, therefore, determined to employ some person who shall ease me of the drudgery of this business. ****** To correspond with those I love is among my highest gratifications. Letters of friendship require no study; the communications they contain flow with ease, and allowances are expected and made. But this is not the case with those which require research, consideration, and recollection."

Washington was compelled to employ a young gentleman of talents and education to relieve himself of these irksome labors, and to his care such correspondence was afterwards committed. This was Tobias Lear, who remained his private secretary until his death. Many personal narratives have come down to us of the kind reception Washington gave his guests at Mount Vernon, and among them is one from the pen of the late Hon. Elkanah Watson, who visited him in the winter of 1785. He had been the senior partner of Watson & Cassoul in France during the war, and has been already referred to in this sketch as having corresponded with Washington at that time, and sent him a box of Masonic regalia.

"The first evening," says he, "I spent under the wing of; Washington's hospitality, we sat a full hour at table by ourselves without the least interruption, after the family had retired. I was extremely oppressed by a severe cold arid excessive coughing, contracted by the exposure of a harsh winter journey. Ho pressed me to take some remedies, but I declined doing so. As usual after retiring, my coughing increased. When some time had elapsed, the door of my room was gently opened, and on drawing my bed curtains, to my utter astonishment I beheld Washington himself standing at my bedside, with a bowl of hot tea in his hand. I was mortified and distressed beyond expression. This little incident occurring in common life with an ordinary man, would not have been noticed; but as a trait of the benevolence and private virtue of Washington, deserves to be recorded."

As Washington had been unable to attend the festival of the Evangelist in December, his Masonic brethren in Alexandria resolved to give an entertainment for him in the following February, and the lodge directed its secretary to write to him to know when it would be convenient for him to favor them with his company. At a subsequent meeting of the lodge, held on the 20th of February, the Worshipful Master, Mr. Adam, informed the brethren that it had been intimated to him that it would be inconvenient for Washington to attend at present, and the invitation was postponed.

On the approach of the festival of St. John the Baptist in June, the lodge addressed Washington an invitation to join them, to which he sent the following reply:

"Mount Vernon, June 19, 1784.
"Dear Sir—With pleasure, I received the invitation of the master and members of Lodge No. 39, to dine with them on the approaching anniversary of St. John the Baptist. If nothing unforeseen at present interferes, I will have the honor of doing it. For the polite and flattering terms in which you have expressed their wishes, you will please accept my thanks.
"With esteem and respect,
"I am, dear sir,
"Your most ob't serv't,
"Go. Washington.
"Wm. Herbert, Esquire."

The records of the lodge, which are still extant, accordingly show that Washington attended as a Mason this festival; and that its Master, Robert Adam, read to the lodge a most instructive lecture on the rise, progress, and advantages of Masonry, and concluded with a prayer suitable to the occasion. The Master and brethren then proceeded to Mr. Weise's tavern, where they dined; and after spending the afternoon in Masonic festivity, returned again to the lodge-room, where, as the record states, "The Worshipful Master, with the unanimous consent of the brethren, was pleased to admit his Excellency General Washington, as an honorary member of Lodge No. 39. Lodge closed in perfect harmony at six o'clock."

In the autumn of 1784, La Fayette came to America, and visited Washington at Mount Vernon. Of all the generals of the Revolution he had been the most beloved by Washington; and both to him and to his wife in France had the hospitalities of Mount Vernon been often tendered by Mr. and Mrs. Washington. Madame La Fayette had wrought with her own hands in France a beautiful Masonic apron of white satin groundwork, with the emblems of Masonry delicately delineated with needlework of colored silk; and this. with some other Masonic ornaments, was placed in a highly finished rosewood box, also beautified with Masonic emblems, and brought to Washington on this occasion as a present by La Fayette. It was a compliment to Washington and to Masonry delicately paid, and remained among the treasures of Mount Vernon till long after its recipient's death, when the apron was presented by his legatees to the Washington Benevolent Society, and by them to the Grand Lodge of Pennsylvania, in whose possession the apron now is, while the box that contained it is in possession of the lodge at Alexandria. The apron presented to Washington by Messrs. Watson & Cassoul two years before, and which is still in possession of Lodge No. 22 at Alexandria, has been often mistaken for this; but the two aprons may be easily identified, by the Watson & Cassoul apron being wrought with gold and silver tissue, with the American and French flags combined upon it, while the La Fayette apron is wrought with silk, and has for its design on the frontlet the Mark Master's circle, and mystic letters, with a *beehive* as its *mark* in the centre.

Masonic Apron of George Washington

The same device is beautifully inlaid on the lid of the box in which it was originally presented to Washington; and as this box is also in possession of Lodge No. 22 at Alexandria, and kept with the Watson & Cassoul apron, it has by many been supposed that this was the apron presented in 1784 by La Fayette. This mistake has also, perhaps, been perpetuated by a statement, that when La Fayette visited this lodge during his visit to America in 1824, he was furnished with the apron now in possession of Lodge No. 22, and in the box in which he had in 1784 presented one to Washington, to wear on the occasion; and that he there alluded to it as the one he had in former years presented to his distinguished American brother. Even were this statement true, a lapse of forty years might have misled him in the identity of the apron, particularly as it was handed to him for the occasion in the well-remembered box in which he had, in his early Masonic life, presented one to Washington. The historic descriptions of the aprons leave no doubt as to the identity of each, and both are among the valued memorials of Washington's Masonic history. The Watson & Cassoul sash and apron, and also the Masonic box in which the La Fayette apron was presented to Washington, were presented to Lodge No. 22, at Alexandria, June 3, 1812, by Major Lawrence Lewis, a nephew of Washington, in behalf of his son, Master Lorenzo Lewis.

Presidential Election
&
Masonic Oath at Inauguration

Washington left his home on the 16th of April, 1789, to repair to New York. At Alexandria, at Georgetown, at Baltimore, at Philadelphia, at Trenton, and at Elizabethtown he was greeted by crowds of his fellow-citizens, who publicly honored him with festivities, civic decorations, and laudatory addresses. He wished to avoid on the occasion all ostentatious display; but the great heart of America was full of love for him, and blessings were showered upon his head, and flowers strown along his pathway.

These various public demonstrations are recorded on the pages of our country's history, and need not be repeated here. It was as if he were passing through the spring fields of a country where tender plants, whose buds had been crushed by war, were now putting forth blossoms, to hide the blood stains that had been left there during the War of the Revolution.

Washington reached New York on the 23d of April, and the 30th of the same month was the day fixed for his inauguration. On that occasion, General Jacob Morton was marshal of the day. He was the Master of St. John's, the oldest lodge in the city, and at the same time Grand Secretary of the Grand Lodge of New York. General Morton brought from the altar of his lodge the Bible with its cushion of crimson velvet, and upon that sacred volume, Robert R. Livingston, Chancellor of the State of New York, and Grand Master of its Grand Lodge, administered to Washington his oath of office as President of the United States.

Having taken the oath, Washington reverently bowed and kissed the sacred volume; and the awful suspense of the moment was broken by Chancellor Livingston, who solemnly said, *"Long Live George Washington, President of the United States!"* A thousand tongues at once joined in repeated acclamations, "LONG LIVE GEORGE WASHINGTON!"

A memorial leaf of the sacred Book was then folded at the page on which Washington had devoutly impressed his lips; and the volume was returned to St. John's Lodge, and placed again upon its sacred altar, A few years later it was again taken from its resting place, and borne in a solemn procession by the Masonic brethren of New York city, who met to pay funeral honors to the memory of Washington.

Bible on Which Washington Took Oath of Office

It is still in possession of St. John's Lodge No. 1, who value it highly as a sacred memento. The memory of Washington's oath of office upon it, is perpetuated by the following inscription, beautifully engrossed, and accompanied by a miniature likeness from an engraving by Leney, which were inserted by order of the lodge. The closing poetic lines were first written by the Rev. Dr. Haven, of Portsmouth, New Hampshire, on Washington's visit to that town in 1789, in answer to an inquiry by what title he should be addressed. The committee appointed by the lodge to form this memorial, were sworn on the same volume to do it faithfully.

ON THIS
SACRED VOLUME,

ON THE 30TH DAY OF APRIL, A.M. 5789, IN THE CITY OF NEW YORK,

WAS ADMINISTERED TO

GEORGE WASHINGTON,

THE FIRST PRESIDENT OF THE UNITED STATES OF AMERICA,

THE OATH

TO SUPPORT THE CONSTITUTION OF THE UNITED STATES.

THIS IMPORTANT CEREMONY WAS PERFORMED BY THE MOST WORSHIPFUL

GRAND MASTER

OF FREE AND ACCEPTED MASONS OF THE STATE OF NEW YORK,

ROBERT R. LIVINGSTON,

CHANCELLOR OF THE STATE.

"Fame spread her wings, and loud her trumpet blew:
Great Washington is near! What praise His due?
What TITLE shall he have? She paused—and said,
Not ONE; HIS NAME ALONE STRIKES EVERY TITLE DEAD!"

Having taken his oath of inauguration, Washington proceeded to the Senate chamber and delivered his first address as chief magistrate of the Federal Union. It was a reflex of the principles of Masonry from the mind and the heart of our greatest American brother. He seemed to imagine himself again treading the ground floor of a new apartment in the temple of human life; and he modestly reviewed his qualifications, his hopes, and fears upon entering it. He next acknowledged a Divine Ruler over all human events, and humbly invoked his guidance and blessing. Was not this a remembrance of the first lessons he had been taught in Masonry? Then, as the Mason examines the lines on his trestle-board, he proceeded to examine the requirements of the constitution, and the duties to be performed under it, and closed with a renewed acknowledgment of dependence on Divine aid. How true was all this to the character of Washington! How true to the teachings of Masonry!

As soon as these ceremonies and duties were performed, President Washington and both houses of Congress proceeded to St. Paul's Church, where divine services were held on the occasion, and the evening was spent by the citizens of New York with the most extravagant exhibitions of joy. A magnificent transparent painting, brilliantly illuminated, was suspended between the fort and Bowling Green, on the centre of which was represented Washington as the emblem of Fortitude; on his right hand, the supreme judiciary, by the emblem of Justice; and on his left, the supreme legislature, by the emblem of Wisdom.

The choice of these emblems from the chambers of Masonic science, and their appropriation at this time to these purposes, must have called the mind of Washington and his Masonic brethren forcibly back to the silent teachings of these very emblems in the lodge-room. Our Federal Government, of which Washington was the representative head, had that day passed a threshold where fortitude, which shrinks at no pain or danger, is required; and he that day stood, as he had long before, and will ever be remembered, a personification of this cardinal Masonic virtue.

It was not until the 16th of May, that answers were returned by the Senate and House of Representatives to Washington's inaugural address; and on such presentations, a question arose between those bodies as to the title by which he should be addressed; the lower body contending that as the constitution fixed no title beyond that of *"The President"* etc., no other should be used; while the Senate preferred to prefix *"His Highness"* or some other title of rank to his name and office. The republican simplicity of the lower house prevailed, and, as is well known, our presidents have ever been addressed without any addition to the title which the constitution gives them.

While this question of courtly official address was occupying the attention of Congress, a kindred one of greater importance and real necessity was forced upon the decision of Washington. It was the etiquette of presidential receptions of citizens and strangers. To establish such rules of private intercourse as these demanded, and still leave the President in command of time necessary for the fulfillment of his official duties, without encroaching upon the claims of nature for rest and refreshment, was a delicate duty for him to perform. There were those who believed that the dignity of the presidential office should be invested with many forms and courtly ceremonies; and there were others who claimed that the harmony of our new-born republican institutions required an entire abandonment of all distinction between the President and the people in social intercourse. The first were, perhaps, too fond of official show, and the latter too anxious for an unbecoming agrarianism. Washington committed the details of presidential etiquette to Colonel David Humphrey, who had been one of his aids-de-camp during the Revolution, and was now his private secretary. Colonel Humphrey seems to have happily conceived appropriate rules and ceremonials for presidential intercourse; for they have remained substantially the same through each successive presidency for three-quarters of a century.

We have already noted in this sketch feelings of jealousy that arose in certain minds relative to the Society of the Cincinnati. These were again aroused by the necessary restrictions that were placed on citizens who sought interviews with the President. Many saw in them only the hated forms and ceremonies of royalty; and Washington was by some denounced as another Royal George. Trifling as such jealousies and fears may now seem to us, they even entered into the political discussions of that day; and a letter is still extant from Washington explanatory of the necessity of the restrictions of the presidential etiquette.

Washington returned to Mount Vernon on the 12th of June, having performed a journey of more than seventeen hundred miles in sixty-six days with his own horses and carriage. He had in that time visited each of the States south of the Potomac, and been received by all classes of citizens with the highest honors.

During his absence his lodge at Alexandria had performed a public labor, in the ceremonials of erecting the first corner-stone of the District of Columbia near that city. As this Federal territory was required, by an act of Congress, to embrace a district of country ten miles square, lying on both sides of the Potomac, Washington had appointed commissioners to establish its boundaries, and its south-east corner-stone was set with Masonic ceremonies on the 15th of April, 1791. Its location was at Jones' Point near the mouth of Hunting Creek, on the bank of the Potomac, near where the Light-house at Alexandria now stands. The following account of setting this stone was written by a gentleman of Alexandria, and published in the United States Gazette at Philadelphia, April 30, 1791:

"Alexandria, April 21, 1791.
"On Friday, the 15th instant, the Hon. Daniel Carroll and Hon. David Steuart arrived in this town to superintend the fixing of the first corner-stone of the Federal District.

"The mayor and commonalty, together with the members of the different lodges of the town, at three o'clock waited on the commissioners at Mr. Weise's, where they dined; and after drinking a glass of wine to the following sentiment viz., 'May the stone which we are about to place in the ground, remain an immovable monument of the wisdom and unanimity of North America'—the company proceeded to Jones' Point in the following order:

"1st. The Town Sergeant.
"2d. Hon. Daniel Carroll and the Mayor.
"3d. Mr. Ellicott and the Recorder.
"4th. Such of the Common Council and Aldermen as were not Freemasons.
"5th. Strangers.
"6th. The Master of Lodge No. 22, with Dr. David Steuart on his right, and the Rev. James Muir on his left, followed by the rest of the Fraternity in their usual form of procession.
"*Lastly*. The citizens, two by two.

"When Mr. Ellicott had ascertained the precise point from which the first line of the district was to proceed, the Master of the lodge and Dr. Steuart, assisted by others of their brethren, placed the stone. After which a deposit of corn, wine, and oil was made upon it, and the following observations were made by the Rev. James Muir:

"'Of America it may be said, as of Judea of old, that it is a good land and large, a land of brooks of waters, of fountains, and depths that spring out of the valleys and hills,—a land of wheat, and barley, and vines, and fig-trees, and pomegranates,—a land of oil, olives, and honey,—a land wherein we eat bread without scarceness, and have lack of nothing,—a land whose stones are iron, and out of whose hills thou mayest dig brass,—a land which the Lord thy God careth for;—the eyes of the Lord thy God are always upon it, from the beginning of the year even unto the end of the year.

"'May Americans be grateful and virtuous, and they shall insure the indulgence of Providence. May they be unanimous and just, and they shall rise to greatness. May true patriotism actuate every heart. May it be the devout and universal wish: Peace be within thy walls, America, and prosperity within thy palaces. Amiable it is for brethren to dwell together in unity; it is more fragrant than the perfumes on Aaron's garment; it is more refreshing than the dews on Hermon's Hill.

"'May this stone long commemorate the goodness of God in those uncommon events which have given America a name among nations. Under this stone may jealousy and selfishness be forever buried. From this stone may a super-structure arise, whose glory, whose magnificence, whose stability, unequalled hitherto, shall astonish the world, and invite even the savage of the wilderness to take shelter under its roof.'

"The company partook of some refreshments, and then returned to the place from whence they came, where a number of toasts were drank; and the following was delivered by the Master of the lodge (Dr. Dick), and was received with every token of approbation:

"BRETHREN AND GENTLEMEN—May Jealousy, that green-eyed monster, be buried deep under the work which we have this day completed, never to rise again within the Federal District.
"It may fairly be presumed that this, or a similar sentiment pervaded the breast of every individual present on the occasion."

These Masonic incidents are of interest, not only to the personal history of Washington, but to both the general and Masonic history of those times. It is well known that Washington directed the tide of events that established the seat of the Federal Government on the Potomac; and that when the act was being passed for its location there, jealousies were aroused within the district on the subject of its boundaries, and the location of its public buildings. Georgetown and Alexandria were both rivals for the honors and advantages incident to their location; and when Washington gave his influence for placing the Capitol on the north side of the Potomac, he yielded his private interest to allay all Northern jealousies as to its location. But the sentiment in Alexandria was adverse to this; and it was befitting Masonry, in the character of Washington's own lodge, to perform the ceremonials in the first public act of establishing the boundaries of the Federal District. Her voice was then, as it ever is, "Let public jealousies be forever buried." Would that her voice were always heeded!
The future seat of the Federal Government had at that time no name, and Mr. Wolcott, of Connecticut, facetiously termed it, "The Indian place, with the long

name on the Potomac," in reference to its Indian name having been *Conecogeague*. It was at first called "The Federal City," and Washington thus styled it in a letter written April 13, 1791; but the commissioners appointed to superintend the laying out of the city, had employed Major L'Enfant, a French architect, to form plans and drawings of it; and in a letter to him, bearing date September 9, 1791, they informed him that they had agreed that the Federal District should be called "The Territory of Columbia," and the Federal City, "The City of Washington," and directed him to thus designate them on his maps.

Laying of the *Southeast* Cornerstone of the U.S. Capitol & Masonic Ceremony

Washington desired to return again to private life at the close of his first presidential term, but having been unanimously re-elected, he yielded to the public wish and the strong solicitations of his friends, and again accepted the presidency. His second inauguration took place in the Senate chamber in Philadelphia, on the 4th of March, 1793. Judge Cushing, of Massachusetts, administered to him the oath of office.

On the 18th of September of that year Washington laid the corner-stone of the Capitol of the United States, in the city that bore his name. It was laid at the southeast corner of the edifice, it being the custom of our Masonic fathers to place it at that point, and not at the northeast as at present. The following account of the ceremonies on the occasion was published in the newspapers of that day.

"Georgetown, September 21, 1793.

"On Wednesday one of the grandest Masonic processions took place, for the purpose of laying the corner-stone of the Capitol of the United States, which, perhaps, was ever exhibited on the like important occasion. About ten o'clock, Lodge No. 9 was visited by that congregation so graceful to the Craft, Lodge No. 22 of Virginia, with all their officers and regalia; and directly afterwards appeared on the southern banks of the grand river Potomac, one of the finest companies of volunteer artillery that hath been lately seen, parading to receive the President of the United States, who shortly came in sight with his suit, to whom the artillery paid their military honors; and his Excellency and suit crossed the Potomac, and was received in Maryland by the officers and brethren of No. 22 Virginia, and No. 9 Maryland, whom the President headed, preceded by a band of music; the rear brought up by the Alexandria volunteer artillery, with grand solemnity of march, proceeded to the President's square, in the city of Washington, where they were met and saluted by No. 15 of the City of Washington in all their elegant badges and clothing, headed by Brother Joseph Clarke, lit. W. G. M., P. T., and conducted to a large lodge prepared for the purpose of their reception. After a short space of time, by the vigilance of Brother Clotworthy Stephenson, Grand Marshal P. T., the brotherhood and other bodies were disposed in a second order of procession, which took place amidst a brilliant crowd of spectators of both sexes, according to the following arrangement, viz.:

Masonic Procession at Laying of Capitol Cornerstone

"The Surveying Department of the City of Washington.

"Mayor and Corporation of Georgetown.

"Virginia Artillery.

"Commissioners of the City of Washington and their attendants.

"Stone-cutters. Mechanics.

"The Sword-bearer.

"Masons of the first degree.

"Bible, etc., on Grand Cushions.

"Deacons, with staffs of office.

"Masons of the second degree.

"Stewards, with wands.

"Masons of the third degree.

"Wardens, with truncheons.

"Secretaries, with tools of office.

"Past Masters, with their regalia.

"Treasurers, with their jewels.

"Band of music.

"Lodge No. 22 of Virginia, disposed, in their own order.

"Corn, Wine, and Oil.

"Grand Master *pro tem.*, Brother George Washington, and Worshipful Master of No. 22 of Virginia,

"Grand Sword-bearer.

"The procession marched two abreast, in the greatest solemn dignity, with music playing, drums beating, colors flying, arid spectators rejoicing, from the President's square to the Capitol in the City of Washington, where the Grand Marshal ordered a halt, and directed each file in the procession to incline two steps, one to the right and one to the left, and face each other, which formed a hollow oblong square, through which the Grand Sword-bearer led the van, followed by the Grand Master P. T. on the left, the President of the United States in the centre, and the Worshipful Master of No. 22 Virginia on the right; all the other orders; that composed the procession advanced in the reverse of their order of march from the President's square to the southeast corner of the Capitol, and the artillery filed off to a destined ground to display their manœuvres and discharge their cannon; the President of the United States, the Grand Master P. T., and the Worshipful Master of No. 22 taking their stand to the east of a large stone, and all the Craft forming a circle westward, stood a short time in awful order.

"The artillery discharged a volley. The Grand Marshal delivered the commissioners a large silver plate with an inscription thereon, which the commissioners ordered to be read, and was as follows:

"This Southeast corner-stone of the Capitol of the United States of America, in the City of Washington, was laid on the 18th day of September, 1793, in the thirteenth year of American independence, in the first year of the second term of the presidency of *George Washington*, whose virtues in the civil administration of his country have been as conspicuous and beneficial, as his military valor and prudence have been useful in establishing her liberties, and in the year of Masonry, 5793, by the President of the United States, in concert with the Grand Lodge of Maryland, several lodges under its jurisdiction, and Lodge No. 22 from Alexandria, Virginia.

"'Thomas Johnson, David Steuart, and Daniel Carroll, Commissioners; Joseph Clarke, K. W. "G. M., P. T.; James Hoban and Stephen Hallate, Architects; Collin Williamson, M. Mason.'

"The artillery discharged a volley. The plate was then delivered to the President, who, attended by the Grand Master P. T., and three most Worshipful Masters, descended to the cavazion trench and deposed the plate, and laid it on the corner-stone of the Capitol of the United States of America, on which was deposed Corn, Wine, and Oil, when the whole congregation joined in reverential prayer, which was succeeded by Masonic chanting honors, and a volley from the artillery.

"The President of the United States and his attendant brethren ascended from the cavazion to the east of the corner-stone; and there the Grand Master P. T., elevated on a triple rostrum, delivered an oration fitting the occasion, which was received with brotherly love and commendation. At intervals, during the delivery of the oration, several volleys were discharged by the artillery. The ceremony ended in prayer, Masonic chanting honors, and a 15-volley from the artillery.

"The whole company retired to an extensive booth, where an ox of 500 lbs. weight was barbecued, of which the company generally partook, with every abundance of other recreation. The festival concluded with fifteen successive volleys from the artillery, whose military discipline and manœuvres merit every commendation. Before dark the whole company departed with joyful hopes of the production of their labor."

Ancient Jewel of the Grand Lodge of Maryland

The following is a copy of the address of Joseph Clarke on the occasion, who acted as Grand Master *pro tem*, of the Grand Lodge of Maryland, in the Masonic jurisdiction of which the Federal Capitol was built:

"MY WORTHY BRETHREN—I presume you expect I shall in some measure address you upon this very important occasion, which I confess is a duty incumbent upon me, although quite inadequate to the task, and entirely unprepared; for until high meridian yesterday, I was not solicited, neither had I a conception to have performed this duty. Therefore you will accept my observations with brotherly love; they are, I assure you, sincere, and dictated by a pure Masonic heart, though very brief.

Volley from the Artillery.

"Brothers, I beg leave to disclose to you that I have, and I expect that you also have, every hope that the grand work we have done to-day will be handed down, as well by record as by oral tradition, to as late posterity as the like work of that ever memorable Temple to our order erected by our Grand Master Solomon.

Volley from the Artillery.

"The work we have done to-day, laying the corner-stone of this designed magnificent temple, the Capitol of our extensive and populous States of veteran republicans, States which were recovered, settled, and permanently established by the virtuous achievements and bravery of our most illustrious Brother George Washington—

Volley from the Artillery.

"I say, that we further hope that this work may be remembered for many ages to come, as, a similar work has from the commencement of time to. this remarkable moment; I mean, the work of laying the corner-stone of our ancient, honorable, and sublime order.

Volley from the Artillery.

"We also, hope that the Grand Architect of all men, Freemasons and others, may continue His great gifts of ability to all those concerned, to persevere in raising, not only on this particular corner-stone, but on every other corner-stone already planted in this extensive site for a commercial Federal city edifices so durable with strength and beauty, that with common care and nurture, they may not envy time. And we further hope that the edifices which may he erected in this territory of Columbia, may be numerously inhabited with citizens, to merit every commendation for their virtue, honor, bravery, industry, and arts.

Volley from the Artillery.

"And I hope that our super-excellent order may here be indefatigably laborious, not only to keep in good repair our hallowed dome, but be incessantly industrious to adorn it with the grand theological virtues, faith, hope, and charity, and embellish it with wisdom, strength, and beauty.

Volley from the Artillery.

"My dear brethren, it would be ungrateful, indeed I think impossible, on this occasion not to notice, under the auspices of our most glorious divine Providence, the growth of this extensive city, in so short a period, by the assiduous, indefatigable labor and industry of all those very valuable characters for virtue, honor, industry, and ability, who have had not only the supreme command, but, in every grade.

Volley from the Artillery.

"Brothers, permit me to suggest to your good understandings, if so much can be done by the local assistance of two-fifteenths of these vast States, by such an eminent Leader, excellent Director, Architects, Surveyors, and Mechanics, what ought we to conceive will be done by them, when aided by the remaining thirteen-fifteenths, who will set to work with willing and powerful hands, not in a local and sparing, but in an infinite and loving manner! And in addition thereto, an universality of individuals, like innumerable hives of bees bestowing their industrious labor on this second paradise.

Volley from the Artillery.

"Then, my dear brethren, Architecture, Masonry, Arts, and Commerce will grow with rapidity inconceivable to me; therefore incomparable. Brethren, although I have neither wishes nor pretensions to divination, yet I venture to prophesy, from such intuitive sense, that all I have suggested to you will soon, come to pass; when we shall all hail, Blessed Territory of Columbia, favored land, soon, very soon, indeed, shall the shores of thy peaceful and delightful city be visited by the commercial interests of the united world; then happy thy sons, and thrice happy those whose prudence and foresight have induced them to become thy citizens!

Volley from the Artillery.

"It must, my dear brethren, be evident to all our understandings, that not only nature, but Providence, have marked their intentions in the most indelible manner, to make the seat for the GRAND MARK, the super-excellent emporium for Politics, Commerce, Arts, and Industry of the United States, seated in the very centricity of our Republic, on the banks of one of the noblest rivers in the Universe, sufficiently capacious to erect thereon a city equal, if not superior in magnitude, to any in the world. It boasts, but then very truly, a climate the most serene and salubrious; equal of accession to all the cardinal and intermediate points, as any place that kind nature has formed, even beyond conception of art, wanting no defence, but what is in, and ever will be in, I trust, the intrepidity and bravery of its founder and citizens.

Volley from the Artillery.

"Although it is not the growth of years, yet there is already planted in this garden or nursery of the Arts, and hath blossomed numerous flowers, that bloom with high lustre in their various departments (not to mention its ever-to-be-remembered founder), but its financiers, conductors, projectors, delineators, and executive geniuses without number, and many of them not only brethren of our order, but brothers of superior, excellent, and sublime estimation.

Volley from the Artillery.

"Certainly, my dear "brethren, it must be as grateful to you, as it is to me, to possess the great pleasure of toying the corner-stone, which we hope, expect, and sincerely pray to produce innumerable corner-stones; and that on every one of them may spring edifices, we fervently pray to the Great Grand Master of heaven, earth, and all things, of His immense wisdom, strength, goodness, and mercy, to grant. So mote it be."

Washington, although holding at this time no official rank in Masonry, except that of Past Master of

Lodge No. 22, at Alexandria, clothed himself for the occasion with an apron and other insignia of a Mason, and, as the foregoing account shows, was honored with the chief place in the procession and ceremonies. The gavel which he used on the occasion was ivory, and is now in possession of Lodge No. 9, at Georgetown, which was represented by its officers and members in the procession. No act of Washington was more historic than this, and yet it has found no place on the pages of our country's history. It was he who was first in the hearts of all men, honoring Masonry by his presence as a brother, and sanctioning by his participation as the chief actor in its highest public ceremonies, its claims as an institution worthy of national confidence and regard. And yet the compilers of our country's annals have ignored the fact, or left it unrecorded on their pages, until their silence has been made to testify that Washington disdained to publicly avow himself a Mason. But he stood on that occasion before his brethren and the world as the representative of Solomon of old, who, the Jewish historian says, "laid the foundation of the Temple very deep in the ground; and the materials were strong stones, and such as would resist the force of time." Those who would blot the record of the mystic labors of Washington, would blush at the memory of one wiser than he.

There is no doubt but that this was one of the Masonic incidents in Washington's history which aided in establishing and perpetuating the illusion that he was the official General Grand Master of the United States; and yet, as we have already stated, such an office in American Masonry is only a historic fiction. Many American brethren have at various times advocated such a centralization of Masonic power and dignity; but to Washington only has been accorded the worthiness to hold it. He lived and died the patron *par excellence* of American Masonry; and her voice as spoken by her orators on public occasions, her muse as breathed in her songs and festive toasts, have sometimes appropriated to him a proposed, but never invested title. When another Washington shall enroll his name upon our American records, and engrave his virtues upon our hearts, perhaps then, but not till then, will all accord united Masonic homage to a General American Grand Master.

There is a striking representation of the features and person of Washington at this period of his life, and perhaps the Masonic dress that he wore at the laying of the corner-stone of the Capitol, still in possession of his old lodge, No. 22, at Alexandria. We have given an accurate copy of this almost unknown original portrait of Washington at the commencement of this volume, and we trust the following extracts from the old records of Alexandria Lodge will justify us in so doing:

"August 29, 1793.—Elisha C. Dick, Master. The Worshipful Master informed the lodge that he convened them in consequence of an offer of Mr. Williams to compliment them with the portrait of the President of the United States, provided they make application to him (the President) for that purpose; and upon taking into consideration the proposal of Mr. Williams, they determined that the following address, signed by the officers of the lodge, be immediately forwarded to our illustrious Brother, the President of the United States."

We regret much that we are unable to give the letter or address, as the above record calls it, of the lodge to Washington, and his reply; but they are not recorded, nor do we know that they are preserved, or any copies of them in existence. That the application met with a favorable response is seen from the following tether extracts from the records:

"*October* 25, 1794.—Mr. Williams having offered to the lodge a drawing of our worthy Brother George Washington, President of the United States, the same is received; and in consequence of the trouble and expense Mr. Williams was at in going to and coming from Philadelphia, it is proposed that the members of the lodge pay him fifty dollars, to be raised by voluntary subscription. Brother Gillis having offered to receive the subscriptions, a list of the members, both town and country, is presented him for that purpose."

"*November* 22, 1794.—Received and read a letter from Mr. Williams, portrait painter, praying for further compensation for painting the President's picture. Ordered to lie over till next lodge-night, or until the Worshipful Master returns."

"*December* 20, 1794.—A letter from Mr. Williams was read, praying (as stated last lodge-night) a further compensation for drawing the President's picture. The lodge are of opinion that in the sum of fifty dollars paid him, he has received full compensation for the same. The lodge, moreover, consider the fifty dollars already paid him a mere gratuity, inasmuch as application was made to the President to sit for his portrait at the request of Mr. Williams, who proposed, should the application be successful, to compliment them with his portrait, promising himself great pecuniary advantages by the sale of copies. The lodge having taken into consideration the propriety of paying the fifty dollars for the President's picture by voluntary subscription, have resolved the same shall be paid out of the funds of the lodge."

On the back of the canvas is the following inscription, apparently in the handwriting of Mr. Williams:

"His Excellency George Washington, Esquire, President of the United Slates. Aged 64. Williams, *Pinxit ad vivum* in Philadelphia, September 18, 1794."

This portrait was placed in an elegant gilt frame, and hung upon the walls of the lodge-room. Its collar and jewel are those of a Past Master, a rank which Washington held in his lodge; and its sash and apron represent those presented to him by Messrs. Watson & Cassoul.

Retirement from Public Life
&
Congratulations from the Grand Lodge of Boston

The closing scene of Washington's administration was on the 4th of March, 1797. Upon the day previous he had given his last presidential dinner, at which many official dignitaries and personal friends were present. On this occasion when the cloth was removed, he took a glass of wine, and raising it to his lips, said: "Ladies and gentlemen, this is the last time I shall drink your health as a public man. I do it with sincerity, wishing you all possible happiness." There was profound silence when this toast was drank, and tears stained the cheeks of many guests at the farewell dinner of Washington.

Washington's administration closed on the following day, and Mr. Adams was inaugurated his successor. On this occasion he publicly appeared for the last time as President, and having introduced Mr. Adams to the assemblage before him, he read to them a brief valedictory which he had prepared. His parting words met with responsive sobs from the audience, and his own great heart swelled with emotions till the tears fell from his cheeks. As he retired from the scene before him, he was followed by a multitude of citizens, all eager to catch the last look of one they loved so well. At his own door he turned to express his acknowledgment to the people; but his voice failed him, and it was only by a wave of his hand that he could convey a farewell blessing.

Washington left Philadelphia in a few days and returned to Mount Vernon, where he at once engaged in superintending the improvement of his estate, and arranging his domestic affairs, which had been neglected during the eight years of his presidency. He had said in a letter to General Knox:

"The remainder of my life, which in the course of nature cannot be long, will' be occupied in rural amusements; and though I shall seclude myself as much as possible from the noisy and bustling crowd, none would more than myself be regaled by the company of those I esteem at Mount Vernon more than twenty miles from which, after I arrive there, it is not likely I shall ever be."

He had scarcely settled himself in his domestic enjoyments, when the voice of Masonry ever grateful to his ear reached him in an address from the Grand Lodge of Massachusetts, which bore date March 21, 1797, of which the following is a copy:

"The *East*, the *West*, and the *South*, of the Grand Lodge of Ancient Free and Accepted Masons, for the Commonwealth of Massachusetts, to their most worthy Brother George Washington.
"Wishing ever to be foremost in testimonials of respect and admiration of those virtues and services with which you have so long adorned and benefited our common country, and not the last nor least to regret the cessation of them in the public councils of the Union, your brethren of this Grand Lodge embrace the earliest opportunity of greeting you in the calm retirement you have contemplated to yourself.
"Though as citizens they lose you in the active labors of political life, they hope as Masons to find you in the pleasing sphere of fraternal engagement. From

the cares of State, and the fatigues of public business, our institution opens a recess, affording all the relief of tranquility, the harmony of peace, and the refreshment of pleasure. Of these may you partake in all their purity and satisfaction; and we will assure ourselves that your attachment to this social plan will increase; and that, under the auspices of your encouragement, assistance, and patronage, the Craft will attain its highest ornament, perfection, and praise. And it is our earnest prayer, that when your light shall be no more visible in this earthly Temple, you may be raised to the *All Perfect Lodge* above, be seated on the right of the Supreme Architect of the Universe, and receive the refreshment your labors have merited.

"In behalf of the Grand Lodge, we subscribe ourselves, with the highest esteem, your affectionate brethren,

"Paul Revere, Grand Master.
"Isaiah Thomas, Senior Grand Warden.
"Joseph Laughton, Junior Grand Warden.
"Daniel Oliver, Grand Secretary.
"Boston, March 21, 5797."

To this address Washington returned the following reply, which was communicated to the Grand Lodge on the 12th of the following June:

"TO THE GRAND LODGE OF ANCIENT FREE AND ACCEPTED MASONS IN THE COMMONWEALTH OF MASSACHUSETTS:

"BROTHERS—It was not until within these few days that I have been favored by the receipt of your affectionate address, dated in Boston, the 21st March.

"For the favorable sentiments you have been pleased to express on the occasion of my past services, and for the regrets with which they are accompanied for the cessation of my public functions, I pray you to accept my best acknowledgments and gratitude.

"No pleasure, except that which results from a consciousness of having, to the utmost of my abilities, discharged the trusts which have been reposed in me by my country, can equal the satisfaction I feel for the unequivocal proofs I continually receive of its approbation of my public con- duct; and I beg you to be assured that the evidence thereof, which is exhibited by the Grand Lodge of Massachusetts, is not among the least pleasing or grateful to my feelings.

"In that retirement which declining years induces me to seek, and which repose, to a mind long employed in public concerns, rendered necessary, my wishes that bounteous Providence will continue to bless and preserve our country in peace, and in the prosperity it has enjoyed, will be warm and sincere; and my attachment to the Society of which we are members will dispose me always to contribute my best endeavors to promote the honor and interest of the Craft.

"For the prayer you offer in my behalf, I entreat you to accept the thanks of a grateful heart, with assurances of fraternal regard, and my best wishes for the honor, happiness, and prosperity of all the members of the Grand Lodge of Massachusetts.

"G°. Washington."

Although this Masonic greeting from the Grand Lodge of Massachusetts antedates any other Masonic intercourse on record after his retirement from the presidency; yet before its reception by him, his own lodge at Alexandria also took measures to welcome his return. For this purpose they addressed him the following letter:

"ALEXANDRIA, March 28, 1797.
"MOST RESPECTED BROTHER—Brothers Ramsey and Marsteller wait upon you with a copy of an address which has been prepared by the unanimous desire of the Ancient York Masons of Lodge No. 22. It is their earnest request that you will partake of a dinner with them, and that you will please appoint the time most convenient for you to attend.
"I am, most beloved Brother,
"Your most obd't and humble serv't,
"James Gillis, M.
"General George Washington."

Washington accepted the invitation, and designated the following Saturday as the time when he would meet the brethren of his lodge. The following account of the addresses and ceremonies on the occasion is given in the "Freemasons' Magazine," published in London in June, 1797:

"United States of America,
Alexandria, April 4, 1797.
"In consequence of an invitation from the Ancient York Masons of the Alexandria Lodge No. 22 to General George Washington, he joined the brethren on Saturday last, when the following address was delivered:

"'MOST RESPECTED BROTHER—The Ancient York Masons of Lodge No. 22 offer you their warmest congratulations, on your retirement from your useful labors. Under the Supreme Architect of the Universe, you have been the Master Workman in erecting the Temple of Liberty in the West, on the broad basis of equal rights. In your wise administration of the Government of the United States for the space of eight years, you have kept within the compass of our happy constitution, and acted upon the square with foreign nations, and thereby preserved your country in peace, and promoted the prosperity and happiness of your fellow-citizens. And now that you have returned from the labors of public life, to the refreshment of domestic tranquility they ardently pray that you may long enjoy all the happiness which the Terrestrial Lodge can afford, and finally be received to a Celestial Lodge, where love, peace, and harmony forever reign, and cherubim and seraphim shall hail you Brother!

"'By the unanimous desire of Lodge No. 22.
"'James Gillis, Master.
"'General George Washington.'

"To which the following reply was made:

"'BROTHERS OF THE ANCIENT YORK MASONS NO. 22—While my heart acknowledges with brotherly love your affectionate congratulations on my retirement from the arduous toils of past years, my gratitude is no less excited by your kind wishes for my future happiness. If it has pleased the Supreme Architect of the Universe to make me an humble instrument to promote the welfare and happiness of my fellow-men, my exertions have been abundantly recompensed by the kind partiality with which they have been received. And the assurances you give me of your belief that I have acted upon the square in my public capacity, will be among my principal enjoyments in this Terrestrial Lodge.
"'G°. Washington.'

"After this the lodge went in procession from their room to Mr. Albert's tavern, where they partook of an elegant dinner prepared for the occasion, at which the utmost harmony prevailed. The following were the principal toasts:
"1st. Prosperity to the Most Ancient and Honorable

Craft.

"2d. All those who live within the Compass and the Square.

"3d. The Temple of Liberty may its pillars be the poles, its canopy the heavens, and its votaries all mankind.

"4th. The virtuous nine.

"5th. The United States of America.

"6th. The Grand Master of Virginia.

"7th. All oppressed and distressed, wherever dispersed.

"8th. Masons' wives, and Masons' barns, and all who wish to lie in Masons' arms.

"9th. May brotherly love unite all nations.
(By Brother Washington.)

"10th. The Lodge at Alexandria, and all Masons throughout the world.

"After which he retired.

"11th. Our most respected Brother George Washington.
Which was drunk with all Masonic honors."

These Masonic incidents in Washington's life occurred while lie was busily preparing to rearrange the domestic concerns of his estate, which had been somewhat neglected during the presidency. In a letter to a friend he says:

"I find myself in the situation of a new beginner; for although I have not houses to build (except one which I must erect for the accommodation and security of my military, civil, and private papers, which are voluminous, and may be interesting), yet I have scarcely any thing else about me that does not require considerable repairs. In a word, I am already surrounded with joiners, masons, and painters; and such is my anxiety to get out of their hands, that I have scarcely a room to put a friend into or to sit in myself, without the music of hammers or the odoriferous smell of paint."

The Illuminati
&
Washington's Fame as a Mason

But Washington was not permitted to enjoy the quietness of Mount Vernon undisturbed by public cares. Before his administration had closed, the government of France assumed an unpleasant position towards our own, and the clouds of war were again gathering thick above our horizon, and threatening to burst upon our country with all their complicated gloom. So imminent had the danger become, that in 1798 a provisional army was ordered to be raised, and all eyes in America were turned on Washington as its commander. He received and reluctantly accepted the appointment, and in the fall of that year again left his own quiet home and repaired to Philadelphia to arrange the details of a perfect military organization of the country for the anticipated contest. While he was engaged in these duties, he received from the Grand Lodge of the State of Maryland a copy of its Book of Constitutions, which had been published the previous year, accompanied by a letter from that Grand Lodge, to which he returned the following reply, dated November 8, 1798:

"To the Right Worshipful Grand Lodge of Freemasons of the State of Maryland:
"Brethren and Brothers—Your obliging and affectionate letter, together with a copy of the Constitutions of Masonry has been put in my hands by your Grand Master, for which, I pray you, to accept my best thanks. So far as I am acquainted with the

principles and doctrines of Freemasonry, I conceive them to be founded on benevolence, and to be exercised only for the good of mankind. I cannot, therefore, upon this ground, withdraw my approbation from it. While I offer my grateful acknowledgments for your congratulations on my late appointment, and for the favorable sentiments you are pleased to express of my conduct, permit me to observe, that, at this important and critical moment, when high and repeated indignities have been offered to the Government of our country, and when the property of our citizens is plundered without a prospect of redress, I conceive it to be the indispensable duty of every American, let his station and circumstances in life be what they may, to come forward in support of the Government of his choice, and to give all the aid in his power towards maintaining that independence which we have' so dearly purchased; and, under this impression, I did not hesitate to lay aside all personal considerations and accept my appointment.

"I pray you to be assured that I receive with gratitude your kind wishes for my health and happiness, and reciprocate them with sincerity.

"I am, gentlemen and brothers, very respectfully,
"Your most obed't serv't,
"G°. Washington."
"November 8, 1798."

The student of Masonic history will remember that this reply from Washington to the Grand Lodge of Maryland was written when our country was agitated with a threatened war with France; and that the intestine commotions that had distracted that republic, were ascribed to the influence of German and French "illuminism," which a Barruel and Robison asserted had been planted and fostered there through the influence of Masonic lodges.

Barruel who was a French Jesuit, used all his professional cunning to implicate Masonry in the excesses of the Jacobins of France and Robison, who was a Scotchman of some literary notoriety, had each issued a work in which they sought to demonstrate that Masonic lodges were all schools of illuminism, in which infidelity and red-republicanism were taught. These works had just made their appearance in this country, and the excesses of the French at home, and their hostile and insolent attitude to our Government, caused them to receive an attention and make an impression on the public mind which would have been impossible under other circumstances. It is worthy of note that the author of one of these productions was a Papist, and that of the other a Scotch Presbyterian.

Masonic lodges in this country had multiplied since the Revolution to an extent unknown before; their membership embraced men in all the honorable walks of life, and higher organizations and Masonic grades of office were being formed in many of the States. Robison had openly asserted that illuminism was a grade in Masonry, which had already been introduced in the United States; and public agitators in this country sought to identify the infidelity of Germany, and the excesses of France, with Masonry in America.

While the public mind was poisoned with these insinuations, and the country was threatened with an invasion by France, Washington received from a clergyman, by the name of Snyder, who resided at Fredericktown, in Maryland, a copy of Mr. Robison's work, which had just been republished in America, entitled "Proofs of a Conspiracy against all the Religions and Governments of Europe, carried on in the secret meetings of Freemasons, Illuminati, and Heading Societies." The book was also accompanied by the following letter to him from Mr. Snyder:

"SIR—You will, I hope, not think it presumption in a stranger, whose name, perhaps, never reached your ears, to address himself to you, the commanding general of a great nation, I am a German born, and liberally educated in the city of Heidelberg, in the Palatinate of the Rhine. I came to this country in 1716, and felt soon after my arrival a close attachment to the liberty for which these Confederated States then, struggled. The same attachment still remains, not glowing, but burning in my breast. At the same time that I am exulting in the measures adopted by our Government, I feel myself elevated in the idea of my adopted country. I am attached, both from the best of education and mature inquiry and research, to the simple doctrines of Christianity, which I have the honor to teach in public; and I do heartily despise all the cavils of infidelity. Our present time is pregnant with the most shocking evils and calamities, which threaten ruin to our liberty and Government. Secretly the most secret plans are in agitation; plans calculated to ensnare the unwary, to attract the gay and irreligious, and to entice even the well-disposed to combine in the general machine for overturning all government and religion.

"It was some time since that a book fell into my hands, entitled 'Proofs of a Conspiracy, etc.,' by John Robison, which gives a full account of a Society of Freemasons, that distinguishes itself by the name of 'Illuminati,' whose plan is to overturn all government and all religion, even natural, and who endeavor to eradicate every idea of a Supreme Being, and distinguish man from beast by his shape only.

"A thought suggested itself to me that some of the lodges in the United States might have caught the infection, and might cooperate with the Illuminati, or the Jacobine clubs in France.

"Fauchet is mentioned by Robison as a zealous member; and who can doubt Genet and Adet? Have not these; their confidants in this country? They use the same expressions, and are generally men of no religion. Upon serious reflection I was led to think that it might be within your power to prevent the horrid plan from corrupting the brethren of the English lodges over which you preside. I send you the ' Proofs of a Conspiracy,' etc., which, I doubt not, will give you satisfaction, and afford you matter for a train of ideas that may operate to our national felicity. If, however, you have already perused the book, it will not, I trust, be disagreeable to you that I address you with this letter, and the book accompanying it. It proceeded from the sincerity of my heart, and my ardent wishes for the common good.

"May the Supreme Ruler of all things continue you long with us in these perilous times; may He endue you with strength and wisdom to save our country in the threatening storms and gathering clouds of factions and commotions; and after you have completed His work on this terrene spot, may He bring you to the full possession of the glorious liberty of the children of God, is the hearty and most sincere wish of
    "Your Excellency's
        "Very humble and devoted servant,
            "G. W. Snyder.
"His Excellency General George Washington.
  "Fredericktown, Maryland, August 22, 1798."

To this letter Washington replied as follows:

  "MOUNT VERNON, 25th September, 1798.
  "THE REV. MR. SNYDER: Sir—Many apologies are due to you for my not acknowledging the receipt of your obliging favor of the 22d ult., and not thanking you, at

an earlier period, for the book you had the goodness to send me.

"I have heard much of the nefarious and dangerous plan and doctrines of the Illuminati, but never saw the book until you were pleased to send it to me. The same causes which have prevented my acknowledging the receipt of your letter have prevented my reading the book hitherto namely, the multiplicity of matters which pressed upon me before, and the debilitated state in which I was left after a severe fever had been removed, and which allows me to add but little more than thanks for your kind wishes and favorable sentiments, except to correct an error you have run into, of my presiding over the English lodges in this country. The fact is, I preside over none, nor have I been in one more than once or twice within the last thirty years. I believe, notwithstanding, that none of the lodges in this country are contaminated with the principles ascribed to the society of the Illuminati.

"With respect, I am, sir,
"Your obedient, humble servant,
"G⁰. Washington."

Mr. Snyder wrote a second letter to Washington, in the following month, on the same subject; and for this we have also made strict search in the archives of the Federal State Department, where the Washington papers are deposited; but it is nowhere to be found. A copy of Washington's reply to this second letter, however, we are able to lay before our readers.

"MOUNT VERNON, 24th October, 1798.
"REVEREND SIR—I have your favor of the 17th instant before me, and my only motive for troubling you with the receipt of the letter is to explain and correct a mistake which, I believe, the hurry in which I am obliged often to write letters has led you into.

"It was not my intention to doubt that the doctrines of the *Illuminati,* and the principles of *Jacobinism* had not spread in the United States. On the contrary, no one is more fully satisfied of this fact than I am.

"The idea I meant to convey was, that I did not believe that the lodges of Freemasons in this country had, as societies, endeavored to propagate the diabolical tenets of the former, or the pernicious principles of the latter, if they are susceptible of separation. That individuals of them may have done it, or that the founder, or instruments employed to found, the democratic societies in the United States may have had these objects, and actually had a separation of the people from their Government in view, is too evident to be questioned.

"My occupations are such that little leisure is allowed me to read newspapers or books of any kind. The reading of letters and preparing answers absorbs much of my time

"With respect, I remain, sir, etc.,

"G°. Washington"

The first letter of General Washington to Mr. Snyder has been often quoted, in some of its parts, to attempt to show that Washington disclaimed all connection with Masonry during his mature and latter years. His statement, that he presided over none of the English lodges of this country, nor had been in one more than once or twice in the last thirty years, is given as if the qualifying designation of English lodges was not there written and fully meant by him. It is well known, as any fact in history, that previous to the Revolution all regular lodges of Masons in this country derived their authority, either directly or indirectly, from one of the Grand Lodges of Great Britain, and Masonry in this country was known as English Masonry, in contradistinction to some of the existing systems of

Continental Europe. When the independence of the United States was fully confirmed, Masonry, as an institution, conformed its organizations and government to the new existing political state of the country; and its lodges, with but few exceptions, relinquished all dependence on their English progenitor and head. American lodges, therefore, in 1798, were as distinct from English lodges, as the independent States were from their former colonial dependence, except in a few instances, where individual lodges, like St. Andrew's in Boston, still continued their fealty to the foreign Grand Lodge, to which they owed their birth, and declined to acknowledge the supremacy or legitimacy of any independent American Grand Lodge. Some of these lodges thus continued until after the commencement of the present century.

There were also many lodges in America, while the Provincial Grand Lodge system was in vogue here, which had their warrants from the Grand Lodges of England direct, and were never, subject to the government of the American Provincial Grand Bodies; and there were other English Military Lodges in this country, both during the Revolution and previous to it, which had no connection with the Provincial Grand Lodges in America, except in owing a common allegiance to the English Grand Easts, from which they sprung. In which of these Washington may "once or twice" have been, we have no record to determine, while we have abundant records to show that he often met with his American brethren in their lodges, and was to the close of his life an affiliated member, and as such received Masonic burial at their hands.

Mr. Snyder was not the only clergyman in America whose fears were aroused by the artful statements of Mr. Robison's book, for it pervaded to a great extent among the Scotch Presbyterians; and in New England many of all classes suffered themselves to be very much alarmed by its statements. Mr. Adams, as President of the United States, had recommended a national fast-day to be observed on the 9th of May, 1798; and on that occasion many clergymen introduced the subject of Illuminism into their discourses, and attempted to show from the writings of Barruel and Robison, that Masonry was an institution dangerous to civil and religious liberty. Much feeling was aroused in New England by these discourses, and the fears of many were excited that Masonry in this country was about to work the same evils here that had been falsely attributed to it in Europe.

To counteract this false impression on the public mind, the Grand Lodge of Massachusetts, at their session on the 11th of June of that year, addressed the following communication to John Adams, as President of the United States:

"Boston, June 11, 1798.
"To the President of the United States:
"Sir—Flattery and a discussion of political opinions are inconsistent with the principles of our Fraternity; but while we are bound to cultivate benevolence, and extend the arm of charity to our brethren of every clime, we feel the strongest obligations to support the civil authority which protects us. And when the illiberal attacks of a foreign enthusiast, aided by the unfounded prejudices of his followers, are tending to embarrass the public mind with respect to the real views of our society, we think it our duty to join in full concert with our fellow-citizens in expressing our gratitude to the Supreme Architect of the Universe, for endowing you with that wisdom, patriotism, firmness, and integrity which has characterized your public conduct.

"While the independence of our country, and the operation of just and equal laws, have contributed to enlarge the sphere of social happiness, we rejoice that our Masonic brethren throughout the United States have discovered by their conduct a zeal to promote the public welfare, and that many of them have been conspicuous for their talents and unwearied exertions. Among those, your *venerable predecessor* is the most illustrious example; and the memory of our beloved Warren, who from the chair of this Grand Lodge has often urged the members to the exercise of patriotism and philanthropy, and who sealed his principles with his blood, shall ever animate us to a laudable imitation of his virtues.

"Sincerely we deprecate the calamities of war, and have fervently wished success to every endeavor for the preservation of peace. But, sir, if we disregard the blessings of liberty, we are unworthy to enjoy them. In vain have our statesmen labored in their public assemblies and by their midnight tapers; in vain have our mountains and valleys been stained with the blood of our heroes, if we want firmness to repel the assaults of every presumptive invader. And while, as citizens of a Free Republic, we engage our utmost exertions in the cause of our country, and offer our services to protect the fair inheritance of our ancestors, as Masons we will cultivate the precepts of our institution and alleviate the miseries of all who by the fortunes of war, or the ordinary concerns of life, are the objects of our attention.

"Long may you continue a patron of the useful arts, and an ornament to the present generation; may you finish your public labors with an approving conscience, and be gathered to the sepulchers of your co-patriots with the benedictions of your countrymen; and finally, may you be admitted to that celestial temple, where all national distinctions are lost in undissembled friendship and universal peace.

"Josiah Bartlett, Grand Master.
"Samuel Dunn, D. G. Master.
"Joseph Laughton, G. Warden
"WM. Little, G. Warden
"Attest: Daniel Oliver, G. Secretary."

To this address, Mr. Adams sent the following courteous and respectful reply.

"GENTLEMEN—As I never had the honor to be one of your ancient fraternity, I feel myself under the greater obligations to you for your respectful and affectionate address. Many of my best friends have been Masons, and two of these, my professional patron, the learned Gridley, and my intimate friend, your immortal Warren, whose life and death are lessons of patriotism and philanthropy, were Grand Masters. Yet so it has happened, that I never had the felicity to be initiated. Such examples as these, and a greater still in my *venerable predecessor*, would have been sufficient to induce me to hold the Institution and Fraternity in esteem and honor, as favorable to the support of civil authority, if I had not known their love of the fine arts, their delight in hospitality, and devotion to humanity.

"Your indulgent opinion of my conduct, and your benevolent wish for the fortunate termination of my public labors, have my sincere thanks.

"The public engagement of your utmost exertions in the cause of your country, and the offer of your services to protect the fair inheritance of your ancestors, are proofs that you are not chargeable with those designs, the imputation of which, in other parts of the world, has embarrassed the public mind with respect to the real views of your society.

"John Adams. "Philadelphia, June 22, 1798."

Mr. Adams had, a few months previous, received a similar letter from the Grand Master of Maryland, in behalf of the Fraternity of that State, to which ho also replied. From this letter and reply, we give the following extracts. Mr. Belton, the Grand Master, in his letter, bearing date Baltimore, July 12, 1798, said:

******** "Permit us to offer our most sincere congratulations on an occurrence the most interesting to Americans. We again behold *our* Washington! the glory of his country the boast, the honor of our Society and of mankind, relinquishing in old age the tranquil scene. Summoned by the voice of his country, we again behold the Hero and the Patriot, willing and forward to sacrifice his private ease for her safety! What heart can be so cold, what heart can so languidly move, as not to beat high and strong at the thought of being once more commanded by that highest ornament of the human character our true, ever-beloved Brother George Washington! The name alone will form a sure defence."

To this sentiment Mr. Adams replied under date of July 18, 1798:

****** "With heartfelt satisfaction, I reciprocate your most sincere congratulations on an occasion the most interesting to Americans. No light or trivial cause would have given you the opportunity of beholding your Washington again relinquishing, the tranquil scenes in delicious shades. To complete the character of French philosophy and French policy, at the end of the eighteenth century, it seemed to be necessary to combat this *Patriot* and *Hero*."

These addresses and replies show that Washington's connection with Masonry was as fully recognized at this period by all classes of American citizens as it was proudly claimed by his, brethren, and that the misinterpretation of his views by its enemies had not then been attempted. Even the Rev. Jedediah Morse, who in his fast-day sermon at Boston, on the 9th of May, had entered largely into the spirit of Barruel and Robison, when he permitted the sermon to appear in print a few months later, softened his accusations in a marginal note by saying:

"Judging from the characters in general who compose the Masonic Fraternity in America, at the head of which stands the immortal Washington, and particularly the characters of the Masons in New England, who, as a body, have ever shown themselves firm and decided supporters of civil and religious order, we may presume that this leaven has not found its way into our American lodges, especially in the Eastern States, If it has been introduced among us, it has probably been insinuated through different channels."

Thus was Washington's fame as a Mason publicly acknowledged and unimpeached, even by those of his contemporaries who assailed the integrity and objects of the institution.

Final Year
&
Masonic Burial

The last year of Washington's life was spent in quietness at his home on the Potomac. His duties as lieutenant-general of the Provisional army did not call him into the field for France assumed a more pacific attitude towards our Government, and he was spared the necessity of directing a bloody conflict with our former ally. The 22d of February, 1799, was a gala-day at Mount Vernon. It was Washington's last celebration of his birthday; and on this occasion his adopted daughter, Nelly Custis, was given by him as the bride of his nephew, Lawrence Lewis. She was the daughter of his stepson, John Parke Custis, who died near Yorktown in 1781. His two youngest children, a son and a daughter, as before stated, had on that occasion been adopted by Washington; and of these Nelly was his favorite, and the bridal flower that graced Mount Vernon on his last birthday.

While the States were English colonies, the king's birthday anniversaries were public holidays; and as such, the 4th of June was King George's day with the people: but after the close of the Revolution, the celebration of Washington's birthday took the place of that; and the 22d of February became a festival day in our country. It was thus observed in Alexandria as early as 1784; and the birth-night balls of February 22 d have been successively continued there. We have also seen notices of it in Richmond as early as 1786, and in Philadelphia, 1790. It also became, during Washington's presidency, a Masonic festival. St.

John's Lodge at Newark, New Jersey, kept it as such as early as 1792; and that venerable lodge has, from that time to the present, yearly convened on that day to commemorate the Masonic virtues of Washington. Little did those brethren, who first met to celebrate it as Masons, reflect how many millions in after-years would regard it as

"The gayest festival in all the year."

Even at the yearly festivals of more ancient origin to commemorate the two St. Johns, it had become the custom to remember Washington in one of the standing Masonic toasts at that day. He was also still remembered in published Masonic addresses dedicated to him. One of these, delivered before a special session of the Grand Lodge of Connecticut, at Norwich, on the 24th of June, 1795, by Dr. Samuel Seabury, the first consecrated Bishop in America, bore the following dedication by him to Washington:

"To the Most Worshipful George Washington, President of the United States of America, the following discourse is respectfully inscribed, by his affectionate brother, and most devoted servant,
                            "Samuel Seabury."

It is a curious fact in the Masonic history of our country during Washington's lifetime, that most dedications of Masonic literature were made to him, while other publications also were in some instances thus dedicated. A curious semi-dedication of a quaint pamphlet, by the Rev. Mason L. Weems, an early biographer of Washington, published in 1799, was thus given, which we here reproduce as the last written correspondence with Washington in which

Masonic allusions are made. The pamphlet was entitled,

"The PHILANTHROPIST, or *Political Peace-Maker* between all honest men of both parties. With the recommendation prefixed by George Washington in his own handwriting, by M. L. Weems, Lodge No. 50, Dumfries."

It was prefaced with the following letter to Washington, and a facsimile copy of his reply, which were as follows:

"To His Excellency George Washington, esquire, *Lieutenant-General of the Armies of the United States*:
"MOST HONORED GENERAL—Scarcely was I delivered of this young republican philanthropist before I began, according to good Christian usage, to look about for a suitable godfather for it. My thoughts, presumptuously enough, I confess, instantly fixed upon you, for two reasons: *First,* I was desirous of paying to you (the first benefactor of my country) this little mite of grateful and affectionate respect; and *secondly,* because I well know there exists not, on this side of heaven, the man who will more cordially than General Washington approve of whatever tends to advance the harmony and happiness of Columbia.

"God, *I pray him, grant!* that you may long live to see us all catching from your fair example that reverence for the Eternal Being, that veneration for the laws, that infinite concern for the *national Union,* that unextinguishable love for our country, and that insuperable contempt of pleasures, of dangers, and of death itself, in its service and defence, which have raised you to immortality, and which alone can exalt us to be a GREAT and HAPPY REPUBLIC.

"On the square of Justice, and on the scale of Love, I remain, honored general, your very sincere friend, and Masonic brother, M. L. Weems."

Washington replied:

"Mount Vernon, 29th August, 1799.

"Rev'd Sir—I have been duly favored with your letter of the 20th instant, accompanying 'The Philanthropist.'

"For your politeness in sending the letter, I pray you to receive my best thanks. Much indeed it is to be wished that the sentiments contained in the Pamphlet, and the doctrines it endeavors to inculcate, were more prevalent. Happy would it be for *this country at least*, if they were so But while the passions of mankind are under so little restraint as they are among us, and while there are so many motives and views to bring them into action, we may wish for, but never see the accomplishment of it.

"With respect,
"I am your most obed't humble servant,
"G°. Washington

"The Rev. M. L. Weems."

Washington's last summer and autumn were spent in arranging the minutest details of his domestic affairs and private business. Whether he had a premonition that it was his last year, no one can determine; but like a wise man, he set his house in order. December came, and with its chilling breath and wintry mantle came also the messenger of death for Washington!

His sickness was sudden, short, and painful. It commenced on the evening of Thursday, the 12th of December, as a common cold, with soreness of the throat. Upon the succeeding day the inflammation there had increased, and in the night became alarming. He was urged to send to Alexandria for Dr. Craik, his family physician, but the night was stormy, and his humanity for his servant induced him to defer it until Saturday morning, using, in the mean time, all the usual domestic remedies in such cases. But these were of no avail, and his physicians came too late. It was eleven o'clock on the forenoon of Saturday before Dr. Craik arrived, and the disease had made so alarming a progress, that two eminent consulting physicians, Dr. Dick, of Alexandria, and Dr. Brown, of Port Tobacco, were also sent for. But none of them could afford relief. The chilling hand of death was already upon him. Fully aware that his last mortal hour had come, he met it with a composure of mind that astonished those about him, saying to his physician, who assured him that he had not long to live: "It is well, doctor: I am not afraid to die." Then calmly crossing his arms upon his breast, he closed his eyes, and, with a few shortening breaths, expired without a struggle, between ten and eleven in the evening.

Mrs. Washington was sitting at the time at the foot of the bed, and as his spirit ebbed away, she buried her face in the enfolded curtains and silently prayed that it might peacefully pass. The stillness of the death-chamber was first broken by her words, as she raised her head and asked in a firm and collected, but mournful voice: "Is he gone?" Mr. Lear, who was standing by the bedside, by a motion of his hand, silently signified that he was no more. "'Tis well,' said she in the same voice; "all is now over; I shall soon follow him; I have no more trials to pass through."

Few were present as witnesses of the scene. It was only the domestic circle of his own household, with, perhaps, a few family friends, and his attending physicians who were there. Of these, Dr. Craik, his life-long friend and family physician, and Dr. Dick, were Masons; the latter being at the time the Master of Washington's own lodge at Alexandria. What Masonic requests may have been made to them during his last hours we know not. But it is well known to every Mason, that the mystic rites of a Masonic burial are not performed, except at a brother's request while living, or by desire of his family after his death. It was believed at the time, by intelligent brethren, that Washington had signified that to be his wish; and the holy rites of the Christian Church of which he was a member, and the mystic rites of Masonry, were each performed in their beautiful simplicity at the tomb of this distinguished brother.

At midnight—*the low twelve of Masonry*—the body was taken from the chamber of death to a large drawing-room below, clothed in burial robes. The death dew had been wiped from its brow, and the pale taper at its head threw a flickering light on the marble features where death had set his signet. From midnight until morning there was stillness there. Words were spoken only in whispers, as if accents from human lips would fall discordant on the sleeper's ear. America, too, in that dread interval from midnight to Sabbath morn, lay in slumber, unconscious of her loss. Morning came, and the hurrying footsteps of family friends, who hastened to Mount Vernon, were heard mingling with those that left to carry the tidings of a Nation's loss! My pen cannot describe what followed. A pencil painted it:

Washington in Glory; America in Tears!

During the day a plain mahogany coffin was ordered from Alexandria, and mourning for the family, over- seers, and domestics at Mount Vernon. The funeral was appointed for Wednesday, the 18th, at meridian; and the Rev. Mr. Davis, the Episcopal clergyman at Alexandria, was invited to perform the burial rites of that Church on the occasion. The selection was an appropriate one; for Mr. Davis was not only the rector of Washington's church, but he was also a member of the same Masonic lodge.

The funeral procession and burial ceremonies were arranged by a committee of Lodge No. 22, at Alexandria, consisting of Dr. Elisha Cullen Dick, its Master; Colonel George Deneale, its Senior Warden; and Colonels Charles Little and Charles Simms, who were members. On Monday, the 16th, an emergent meeting of this lodge was called, at which Dr. Dick, its Master, presided. Forty-one of its members were present, and two visiting brethren, one from Fredericksburg, where Washington was made a Mason, and the other from Philadelphia.

Dr. Dick addressed the brethren in a feeling manner, on the event which had called them together. It was their first recorded meeting on an occasion like this. They sat in sorrow there. The death-angel's alarm at their tiled door had found none to withstand his approach, or ask from whence he came, or what he came thither to do. With step unseen, and salutation strange to all, he had approached their midst, removed from before their altar a mystic taper, and taken it to the Grand Lodge above. To arrange for commemorating, in the burial of their departed Washington, the extinguishing of that light in their lodge, and their confident hope of finding it shining with brighter rays before the Grand Orient of the Holy One on High, they were now met.

There was also another Masonic lodge at that time in Alexandria, called Brooke Lodge No. 47, which was convened at the same hour. A committee from No. 22, consisting of Brothers Joseph Neale and Thomas Petrekin was appointed to confer with No. 47; and the joint committee of both lodges agreed upon the ceremonies as arranged by the former committee of Lodge No. 22. There were also two other lodges at that time in the Federal District, held under warrants from the grand Lodge of Maryland. These were Potomac Lodge No. 9, at Georgetown, and Federal Lodge No. 15, at Washington. A messenger was appointed by No. 22 to wait on these lodges on Tuesday, "and invite them to join the funeral procession at Mount Vernon on Wednesday at twelve o'clock, if fair, or on Thursday at the same hour." The deacons of the lodge were directed to have the *Orders* cleaned and prepared, and to furnish spermaceti candles for them. The secretary was also directed to have the case in which the charter was kept repaired and gilded for the occasion. It was also arranged that the military companies of Alexandria should join in the procession as an escort and guard of honor. They were at that time under command of Colonel Deneale, the Senior Warden of Washington's lodge. These arrangements having been signified to the family, Mr. Lear, Washington's late private secretary, ordered, as was the custom at that day, provisions and other refreshments to be provided at Mount Vernon for the funeral assembly.

Upon the next day, Wednesday, December 18th, the citizens about Mount Vernon commenced assembling there at eleven o'clock, and the encoffined body of the illustrious dead was placed in the piazza of the grand old mansion, where, while living, he had been accustomed to walk and muse, or converse with visitors. On an ornament at the head of the coffin was inscribed, SURGE AD JUDICITUM, and beneath it GLORIA DEO; and upon a silver plate on the middle of the lid was inscribed,

GENERAL
GEORGE WASHINGTON
DEPARTED THIS LIFE ON THE 14TH DECEMBER, 1799, ÆT. 68.

The sun had passed its meridian height before the Fraternity and military escort arrived from Alexandria. The Masonic apron and two crossed swords were then placed upon the coffin, a few mystic words were spoken, and the brethren one by one filed by the noble form, majestic even in death, and took a last sad look on one they had loved so well. Alas, the light of his eye and the breathing of his lips in language of fraternal greeting were lost to them forever on this side of the grave!

Adown the shaded avenues that led from the mansion to the Potomac might then be seen a vessel at anchor, with its white sails furled, awaiting the procession's forming. The cavalry took its position in the van, and next came the infantry and guard, all with arms reversed. Behind them followed a small band of music with muffled drums; and next the clergy, two and two. They were four in number viz., the Rev. Dr. Muir and the Rev. Messrs. Davis, Maffit, and Addison the first three of whom were Masons and members of Lodge No. 22, at Alexandria. Then followed Washington's war-horse, led by two grooms dressed in black. It was riderless that day, but carried saddle, holsters, and pistols. Next was placed the body on its bier, covered with a dark pall. Six Masonic brethren attended it as pall-bearers. They were Colonels Gilpin, Marsteller, and Little on the right, and Colonels Simms, Ramsey, and Payne on the left, all members of Washington's own lodge. Each of them wore on his left arm an ample badge of black crape, which may still be seen, together with the bier on which the body was borne, in the Museum at Alexandria. The relatives of the deceased and a few intimate family friends then followed as principal mourners. Then came the officers and members of his lodge and other Masonic brethren, all too as mourners.

The officers of the corporation of Alexandria then took their places behind the Masonic Fraternity; citizens followed, preceded by the overseers of the Mount Vernon estate, and its domestics closed the procession.

It was between three and four o'clock before the procession moved. The booming cannon from the vessel on the river was the signal, and then with slow and measured steps that melted their souls in all the tenderness of woe, their way was taken to the family vault at the bottom of the lawn near the bank of the Potomac. The military escort there halted and formed their lines. The body, the clergy, the mourning relatives, and the Masonic brethren then passed between them, and approached the door of the tomb. There the encoffined Washington rested on his bier before them. Dr. Dick, the Master of the lodge, and the Rev. Thomas Davis, rector of Christ Church, stood at its head, the mourning relatives at its foot, and the Fraternity in a circle around the tomb.

The Rev. Mr. Davis broke the silence by repeating from sacred writings, "I am the resurrection and the life; he that believeth in Me, though he were dead, yet shall he live." Then with bowed and reverent heads all listened to the voice of prayer; and as the holy words went on, as used in the beautiful and expressive burial-service of the Episcopal Church, their soothing spirit was echoed in the responses of the multitude around. Mr. Davis closed his burial-service with a short address. There was a pause; and then the Master of the lodge performed the mystic funeral rites of Masonry, as the last service at the burial of Washington. The apron and the swords were removed from the coffin, for their place was no longer there. It was ready for entombment. The brethren one by one cast upon it an evergreen sprig; and their hearts spoke the Mason's farewell as they bestowed their last mystic gift. There was a breathless silence there during this scene.

Masonic Funeral Ceremonies During Late 1700s

So still was all around in the gathered multitude of citizens, that they might almost have heard the echoes of the acacia ns it fell with from trembling lightness upon the coffin-lid. The pall-bearers placed their precious burden in the tomb's cold embrace, earth was cast on the threshold, and the words were spoken: *"Earth to earth—ashes to ashes—dust to dust!"* and the entombment of Washington was finished. The mystic public burial honors of Masonry were given by each brother with lifted hands, saying in his heart, "Alas! my Brother! *we have knelt with thee in prayer, ice have pressed thee to our bosoms, we will meet thee in heaven!*" The mystic chain was reunited in the circle there, the cannon on the vessel and on the banks above them fired their burial salute, and Mount Vernon's tomb was left in possession of its noblest sleeper. The sun was then setting, and the pall of night mantled the pathway of the Masonic brethren as they sadly returned to their homes.

Lodge No. 22, at Alexandria, had then left on its roll of membership sixty-nine Masons, sixty of whom were Master Masons, and nine Entered Apprentices. It met on the following day in regular communication, and elected Colonel George Deneale its Master. It had presided over while under its Pennsylvania Warrant by three Masters—viz,; Robert Adam, Robert McCrea, and Dr. Dick, Under its Virginia Warrant it had also had the same number—George Washington, James Gillis, and Dr. Dick.

> "Three there were, but one was not,—
> He lay where Cassia mark'd the spot."

It had been the custom of this lodge from its first organization to meet on the festivals of St. John the Evangelist in December and listen to charity sermons, collect contributions for the indigent, and partake of social refreshments. St. John's day in December, 1799, was duly observed, but all hilarity was dispensed with. It was made a mourning day for the loss of Washington. Dr. Dick installed Colonel Deneale as his successor in the chair; but before doing that duty, he addressed the lodge as its retiring Master. Having made the customary demands for charity, he closed by saying in a feeling manner:

"Whilst every recurrence of this festival demands that we distribute a portion of the comforts we possess among those of our more immediate neighbors who are unhappily destitute, it has also, hitherto, invited us to social and convivial enjoyment. After having fulfilled the primary duties of the day, it has been heretofore our custom to indulge in festive gayety; and, indeed, nothing can either so fully sanction such an indulgence, or capacitate the mind for a real and rational enjoyment of it, as the due observance of this preliminary injunction.

"But on the present occasion, my brethren, a cloud of sorrow surrounds our prospects. A recent and heavy calamity has obstructed every avenue to mirth. Our great and good Grand Master is no more! He who hath so often united in our annual celebrations is gone, to return not again. He whose presence was wont to inspire surrounding multitudes with reverence and admiration he who was but lately the boast of his own country and the wonder of the world, now lies cold and prostrate in his tomb! Thus, my brethren, is lost from the treasury of the Universal Lodge its brightest jewel!

"Feeble is the language of eulogium when applied to a character of such uncommon worth. Statues of marble will prove the love and gratitude of his survivors; but his own virtues and his services have already implanted a monument far more durable than these in the bosoms of his countrymen. May it be particularly nurtured by the Fraternity of Free and Accepted Masons to the end of time. So mote it be."

When this address and the ceremonies of installment were concluded, the lodge, accompanied by Lodge No. 47, walked in procession to the Presbyterian Church, where a sermon was preached on the occasion by the Rev. Bro. WM. Maffit, after which they returned to the lodge-room. On the two succeeding Sabbaths the Masonic brethren of Alexandria met in their lodges, clothed themselves in mourning, and repaired in procession to the Presbyterian Church, where sermons on the occasion of Washington's death were preached, on the first by the Rev. Bros. Thomas Davis and Dr. Muir, and on the second by the Rev. Mr. Tollison.

The funeral of Washington at Mount Vernon, and memorial ceremonies at Alexandria, had thus far been conducted by the Masonic Fraternity; but on the 22d of the following February, the citizens there assembled in all their various capacities; Masonic, military, civic, and religious bodies uniting in accordance with a recommendation of Congress, to honor the memory of him whom all had loved, and whose loss all mourned. Lodge No. 22 had, at its meeting on the 20th of this month,

"Resolved, That the members belonging to this lodge wear on the 22d instant, and for thirty days thereafter, a white ribbon through two button-holes on the left side of their coats, and that the columns, orders, and deacon's staffs be shrouded with black; ******* and that the members of this lodge do assemble at our lodge-room precisely at ten o'clock on Saturday, the 22d instant, in order to evince the respect they owe to their late departed brother, General George Washington."

Colonel Deneale, the Master of Lodge No. 22, was selected by the citizens as the officer of the day for the anniversary, and his lodge joined with Brooke Lodge, and united with the military and various other bodies of citizens, and walked through several of the principal streets of Alexandria to the Presbyterian meetinghouse, where Dr. Dick, late Master of Lodge

No. 22, who had been appointed the orator for the occasion, delivered a feeling and eloquent address. We have already given his eulogium before his brethren in the lodge-room, at their first meeting after the funeral of Washington, and we here give an extract from his portraiture of him as a man on this public occasion—a day set apart for a united homage of all American citizens to his memory.

"Four millions of the human race—free in their thoughts and affections, unrestrained in their actions, widely dispersed over an extensive portion of the habitable globe—are seen devoted to a single purpose;—a people detached by local causes; actuated in common life by opposite views, or rivals in the pursuit of similar objects; jealous in all other matters of general concern, are offering the tribute of affection to the memory of their common friend. In vain shall we examine the records of antiquity for its parallel. Worth so transcendent as to merit universal homage, with a correspondent desire to bestow it, mark an event in the history of our country that may be considered as a phenomenon in the annals of man.

"Modest and unassuming, yet dignified in his manners; accessible and communicative, yet superior to familiarity; he inspired and preserved the love and respect of all who knew him. For the promotion of all public and useful undertakings, he was singularly munificent. The indigent and distressed were at all times subjects of his sympathy and concern. His charity flowed in quiet, but constant streams from a fountain that was at no time suffered to sustain the smallest diminution. No pursuit or avocation, however momentous, was permitted to interrupt his systematic attention to the children of want. His anxious solicitude on this score is pathetically exemplified in a letter, written in 1775, at a time when the unorganized state of the army might have demanded his exclusive concern. Addressing himself to the late Washington, he writes: 'Let the hospitality of the house be kept with respect to the poor. Let no one go away hungry. If any of this kind of people should be in want of corn, supply their necessities, provided it does not encourage them in idleness. I have no objection to your giving my money in charity, when you think it will be well bestowed. I mean, that it is my desire that it should be done. You are to consider that neither myself nor my wife are now in the way to do these good offices.'

"Such, my fellow-citizens, was the man whose memory we have assembled to honor. It has been your peculiar felicity often to have seen him on the footing of social intimacy. That the inhabitants of Alexandria held a distinguished place in his affection, you have had repeated testimony. You have seen his sensibility awakened on occasions calculated to call forth a display of his partiality. The last time we met to offer our salutations and express our inviolable attachment to the venerable sage, on his retiring from the chief magistracy of the Union, you may remember that in telling you how peculiarly grateful were your expressions, the visible emotions of his great soul had almost deprived him of the power of utterance.

"But Heaven has reclaimed its treasure, and America has lost its first of patriots and best of men, its shield in war, in peace its brightest ornament; the avenger of its wrongs; the oracle of its wisdom, and the mirror of its perfection. His fair fame, secure in its immortality, shall shine through countless ages with undiminished lustre. It shall be the statesman's polar-star, the hero's destiny, the boast of age, the companion of maturity, and the goal of youth. It shall be the last national office of hoary dotage to teach the infant, that hangs on his trembling knee, to lisp the name of WASHINGTON!"

Masonic records state that prayers were also delivered on this occasion by the Rev. Bros. Dr. Mum, Thomas Davis, and WM. Maffit, after which the brethren returned to their rooms, and the lodge was closed in harmony at three o'clock.

Masonic Reaction After the Death of Washington

Rumor of Washington's death reached Philadelphia, where Congress was sitting, on Wednesday, December 18th, the day of his funeral. The next day the sad news became painfully certain, and was formally announced by the President to Congress. It soon became known in all parts of the country, and produced more profound emotions of sorrow than had been felt by the American people for the loss of any citizen. The great heart of the nation swelled for a moment with grief, and then beat with rapid throbs of unwonted agony. The National Congress, State legislatures, municipal bodies, religious societies, civic and scientific associations, military organizations, and all classes of citizens felt and manifested a common bereavement.

But while these all combined to express their deep sense of the national affliction, two other associations, with which Washington had been intimately connected, joined in the common bewailment with deep expressions of fraternal grief. These were the societies of the Cincinnati and the Masonic Lodges of America. With the Cincinnati, Washington had held from its first organization the highest official membership, and they mourned their chief with processions, eulogies, and sable habiliments suited to the genius of that institution. The Masonic Fraternity, too, had long regarded him as the chief ornament of their society, and wherever funeral ceremonies were held, they joined their fellow-citizens, with their emblems draped in symbolic sorrow, and expressed a mournful remembrance of their loved and departed brother by many ancient and hallowed forms peculiar to their fraternity.

The genius of America lent its aid to express a nation's woe. The artisan gave his cunning skill, the artist all the rich hues of his pencil, the poet all the inspiration of his pen, the orator all his melting pathos, and fancy wove its fairest garlands to express in every varied form one common sorrow; and eulogies and dirges, catafalcos and urns, gave expression to the grief of America at her first great national bereavement.

Congress designated the 26th of December as the day on which a national tribute should be paid by that body to the memory of Washington, and all other public bodies in and about Philadelphia were invited to join on the occasion.' The Masonic Fraternity were assigned a distinguished place in the procession on that day, it being among the chief mourners. Major-General Henry Lee, who was the orator of the day, was himself a Mason and member of Hiram Lodge No. 59, at Westmoreland Court House, Virginia.

The invitation by Congress to the Masonic Fraternity to join in the funeral solemnities having been received by the Grand Master of Pennsylvania, he issued his orders on the 24th, convening his Grand Lodge at ten o'clock on the day appointed. That body accordingly met in extra Grand Communication on that day, and were thus addressed by their Grand Master Jonathan Bayard Smith:

"Right Worshipful Deputy Grand Master, Senior and Junior Grand Wardens, and Brethren. You have been called to hold this special convention in consequence of an invitation to join the representatives of a great and grateful people in a solemn act of duty. With respect to the unexpectedly early moment of executing this duty, we have been anticipated; but by the death of General George Washington, we have felt ourselves impelled, irresistibly impelled, to yield to the strongest emotion of the heart, and cordially to join our fellow-citizens in public evidences of estimation and regret.

"The interesting event having been officially communicated to the public, I immediately directed that the sable emblems of our order should be borne in Grand Lodge by the members at our next communication, then to take place in a few days, wishing to give to ulterior orders on the occasion the force and the dignity of the spontaneous voice of the collected craft of Pennsylvania.

"While we respectfully leave to abler hands, to the appointed organ of the councils of the United States, to the common voice of his country and of mankind, and to succeeding ages, which will venerate his name as long as they shall experience the happy effects of his civic virtues and public services, duly to appreciate his worth, the Masons of Pennsylvania, impressed with their more immediate Masonic connections and character, may be allowed to deplore that their friend, their brother, their father is gone. Yes, my brethren, as such the Masons of Pennsylvania did long ago recognize him. It is now twenty-one years since they, by an unanimous suffrage, proposed him as Grand Master of Masons for the United States. They have on sundry occasions, and very lately, given attestations of unabated attachment to his person, and a high sense of his unremitting endeavors in promoting order, union, and brotherly affection among us, and in carrying forth the principles of the lodge into every walk of life. In our archives are found flattering evidences of his reciprocated esteem and approbation of our order, as relative more especially to those two chiefest concerns of man, religion and government. The public have seen him gracing and dignifying our processions by his attendance. We have been made the almoners and dispensers of his charitable beneficence. But, my brethren, this pleasing intercourse is suspended. Since our last communication, this our brother has been removed from a terrene to expand his ample mind in the boundless duties and enjoyments of a celestial lodge of that eternal temple (to use his own expression to our Grand Lodge), whose builder 'is the Great Architect of the Universe. The Old as well as the New World reveres his name. He was indeed an illustrious brother, citizen, and chief, in peace and in war, in council and in action, pre-eminent. The Masons of Pennsylvania have exulted that the name of Washington stood enrolled on their list of brethren; and they will cherish the remembrance of his virtues and his services as a rich legacy for their emulous example. If devotion of time and talents to ameliorate the state of man be a virtue; if obeying the calls of his country in times of the greatest difficulty and danger, at every risk, be a Masonic duty; of that virtue may Masonry boast that this our Washington has exhibited an instance beyond former example brilliant, and for the exercise of this duty will our Washington ever stand conspicuous in the foremost rank. Is a love of order and sacred regard to the laws of the social compact characteristic of Masons? For his exemplary adherence to these Masonic virtues, through all the vicissitudes and variegated difficulties of a Revolutionary War, has our Washington received the plaudits of thirteen sovereign States.

"It now remains, my brethren, that in our several spheres we do likewise as our brother has done; that by showing respect to merit, it appear that we value it; that by cordial regret on the translation of virtue from among us, we evidence* that we revere it; and while we drop our portion amid the universal effusion of sorrow on this mournful occasion, we anticipate for our lamented brother the applause of nations and the veneration of ages.

"I detain you no longer. The government of our country has this day honorably distinguished us as among the chief mourners of Washington, its friend, its protector, and its ornament. The destined hour has come, and we move to the summons."

It was then:

"*Resolved*, That this Grand Lodge are deeply and sincerely afflicted with the melancholy event which has occasioned this communication, and will immediately proceed to join in the honors about to be shown to the memory of our illustrious deceased brother."

The Grand Master then appointed Colonel Thomas Proctor master of ceremonies for the day. The brethren then formed in due order in the Grand Lodge-room, and moving from thence joined the general procession, which proceeded to Zion Church, where religious services were performed by the Rev. Dr. White, and the oration was delivered by General Lee; after which they returned to the Grand Lodge-room, and their labors for the day were closed.

Upon the following day the Grand Lodge again met, the Grand Master recalled their attention to the mournful occasion of the preceding day, and it was unanimously

"*Resolved*, That the room committee be directed to put the Grand Lodge-room in mourning, in such a manner as they shall conceive to be most suitable and proper to testify our fraternal attachment to our late Brother Washington, and the high veneration we entertain for his memory and virtues.

"*Resolved*, That as a further mark of our warm regard for the memory of our deceased brother, and deep affliction for the loss we have sustained by his death, the members of the Grand Lodge wear black crape on their left arm, as recommended by the President and Congress to the citizens of the United States; and that the emblems on their aprons be covered with black for the term of six months, being until St. John's day next; and that the same be recommended to all the lodges under the jurisdiction of this Grand Lodge."

There existed in Philadelphia at that time, under a warrant from the Grand Lodge of Pennsylvania, a French Lodge of Ancient York Masons, t known as "*L'Aménité*, No. 71." On the following week (January 1, 1800), a *sorrow lodge* was held by these brethren, which was attended by the officers of the Grand Lodge, and a great number of the Fraternity in that city. After the conclusion of ceremonies peculiar to such a lodge, an oration was delivered by its orator, Simon Chaudron, in the French language, which was followed by an address in English by the Master, Joseph de la Grange. This oration was published in both the French and English languages, and copies were sent to the President and Vice-president of the United States, to the governor of Pennsylvania, and to Mrs. Washington at Mount Vernon. They all acknowledged their receipt by letter; and Mrs. Washington's, by the hand of the private secretary of her late husband, was as follows:

"MOUNT VERNON, May 15, 1800.

"SIR—In compliance with Mrs. Washington's request, I have the honor to acknowledge the receipt of your letter to her of the 15th of March, with three copies of the funeral oration which the French Lodge,

L'Aménité, in Philadelphia, have consecrated to the memory of her husband.

"Impressed with a lively sense of this testimonial of respect and veneration paid to the memory of the partner of her heart, Mrs. Washington begs the lodge will be assured of her grateful acknowledgments; and you will be pleased to accept her best thanks for the obliging manner in which you have communicated their sympathy in her affliction and irreparable loss.

"I am, sir,
"Very respectfully,
"Your obedient servant,
"Tobias Lear,
"Secretary to the late General Washington."

The news of Washington's death reached New York on Friday, December 20th. The Common Council on that day publicly announced it to the citizens, and signified to the different religious societies of the city their wish that their churches be draped in mourning, and their bells muffled and tolled every day from twelve till one o'clock until the 24th inclusive.

Upon Monday, the 23d, the Grand Lodge of New York was convened in an extra Grand Communication. General Jacob Morton, the Deputy Grand Master, presided on the occasion, and

"Announced that the reason for convening this extra meeting of the Grand Lodge was, the mournful intelligence of the death of their illustrious and much beloved Brother George Washington, late President of the United States, and commander-in-chief of the army; and urged with energy and respectful expressions the duties which belong to every Mason on such a painful event, and the necessity of this Grand Lodge to take such steps as are proper and Masonic, to pay the tribute of respect due to a brother, who, being called to the Celestial Lodge above, lives in the heart of the virtuous and the wise.

"Whereupon the following was decreed: 'The Grand Lodge, with the deepest and sincerest sorrow, announces to the Lodges under its jurisdiction the death of their illustrious and much beloved Brother George Washington, late President of the United States, and commander-in-chief of its army. He closed his useful and honorable life at his seat at Mount Vernon on the night of the 14th instant, in the 68th year of his age.

"'When, in the dispensations of Providence, the great and the good, when those whom we love and revere sink into the silent tomb, the afflicted heart seeks its solace in rendering to their memories every honorable tribute which affectionate gratitude can devise. This is a feeling engrafted in our natures, as an incentive to honorable ambition; and the expression of those feelings is a duty which the customs of civil society have enjoined; but in decreeing a tribute of respect to our deceased brother on this occasion, there is naught we can devise which will fully evince our veneration of his virtues or our sorrow for his loss.

"'To decree honor to that illustrious name upon which glory hath already exhausted all her store; to render a tribute of affection to his memory who lived in the hearts of a grateful people, are duties which we feel we can never satisfactorily perform. That humble tribute which we are enabled to pay, we decree.

"'*Resolved*, Therefore, that all the lodges under our jurisdiction be clothed in mourning for the space of six months, and that the brethren also wear mourning for the same space of time.

"'Resolved, That a committee be appointed to erect at the expense of this Grand Lodge a monumental memorial to the virtues of our illustrious brother, to be placed in the room occupied by the Grand Lodge for its sittings; and that the Right Worshipful Jacob Morton, Deputy Grand Master; the Right Worshipful Martin Hoffman, Senior Grand Warden; the Right Worshipful Abraham Skinner, Junior Grand Warden; the Right Worshipful Revier John Vanden Broeck, Grand Secretary; and the Worshipful Brethren Cadwalader D. Colden and Peter Irvin be a committee for that purpose.

"'*Resolved*, That the said committee have authority to meet and concur with such other committees of our fellow citizens, as shall be appointed to devise some public testimonials of respect and veneration to the memory of our departed brother.

"'*Resolved*, That the Grand Secretary be directed to write circular letters to the different Grand Lodges in the United States, condoling with them on the loss which we have sustained in the death of our beloved brother, who was the chief ornament of his country, and the pride of our institution.

"'*Resolved*, That the Grand Secretary be directed to forward immediately a copy of these resolutions to the several lodges in this city.'"

In accordance with these resolutions, the Masonic Fraternity joined in the public proceedings held in the city of New York on the 31st of December, to express sorrow at the death of Washington. The place assigned them was among the chief mourners. The Bible on which Washington had taken his first oath of office as President of the United States was borne before the Grand Master, and all the decorations they carried in the procession were mournfully impressive.

They marched to St. Paul's Church, where an oration was delivered by Gouverneub Mobbis, accompanied by appropriate music.

The tidings of Washington's death reached Boston on the 23d of December, during a celebration held that day to commemorate the landing of the Pilgrims in 1620. In the morning a rumor came that Washington was dead! Before noon its truth was confirmed. Common festivals upon such intelligence would have been omitted. But the impressions arising from the celebration were thought not inconsistent with a due sensibility to the sad event which was announced. The usual expressions of gayety had no place, and the guests assembled together rather for condolence than festivity.

On the 28th of this month the following circular was issued by the Grand Master of Massachusetts to the Fraternity in that State:

"GRAND LODGE OF MASSACHUSETTS,
Boston, December 28, A.D. 1799.

[L. s.] "To testify their veneration of the exalted character and pre-eminent virtues, and their respect for the memory of their highly distinguished Brother George Washington, it is recommended to the brethren of the Fraternity of Free and Accepted Masons in the Commonwealth of Massachusetts to wear, for the term of six weeks, commencing on the 1st day of January, 1800, a black crape OD the left arm below the elbow, interwoven with a narrow ribbon running direct.

"By order of the Most Worshipful,
"Samuel Dunn, Esq.,
"Daniel Oliver, *Grand Secretary*."

Some of the lodges in and about Boston solemnized the event of Washington's death, either in their private meetings of by uniting with citizens in public ceremonies soon after this order was given; but the Grand Lodge of that jurisdiction took no steps towards a public testimonial of their respect for his memory until the 15th of the following month (January, 1800), when they resolved to pay funeral honors to his memory on the 22d of February. But finding that the authorities of the General and State governments had also designated that day for public ceremonies in honor of Washington, it was subsequently thought by the Grand Lodge, that distinct Masonic ceremonies were more appropriate for the Fraternity, and they changed the time of their own funeral ceremonies from the 22d to the 11th of February. The Grand Lodge of Massachusetts had, however, previous to this, written a letter of condolence to Mrs. Washington, and solicited a lock of her deceased husband's hair. This she complied with, as the following correspondence shows:

"Boston, January 11, 1800.
"Madam—The Grand Lodge of the Commonwealth of Massachusetts have deeply participated in the general grief of their fellow-citizens, on the melancholy occasion of the death of their beloved Washington.

"As Americans, they have lamented the loss of the chief who led their armies to victory, and their country to glory; but as Masons they have wept the dissolution of that endearing relation by which they were enabled to call him their friend and their brother. They presume not to offer you those consolations which might alleviate the weight of common sorrows, for they are themselves inconsolable. The object of this address is not to interrupt the sacred offices of grief like yours; but whilst they are mingling tears with each other on the common calamity, to condole with you on the irreparable misfortune which you have individually experienced.

"To their expressions of sympathy on this solemn dispensation, the Grand Lodge have subjoined an order, that a Golden Urn be prepared as a deposit for a lock of hair, an invaluable relique of the Hero and the

Patriot whom their wishes would immortalize; and that it be preserved with the jewels and regalia of the society.

"Should this favor be granted, madam, it will be cherished as the most precious jewel in the cabinet of the lodge, as the memory of his virtues will forever be in the hearts of its members. We have the honor to be, with the highest respect, your most obedient servants,

"John Warren,
"Paul Revere,
"Josiah Bartlett.

"Mrs. Martha Washington."

To this request Mrs. Washington replied through Mr. Leah, inclosing a lock of Washington's hair, which was duly received.

"Mount Vernon, January 27, 1800.

"GENTLEMEN—Mrs. Washington has received, with sensibility, your letter of the llth instant, inclosing a vote of the Grand Lodge of Massachusetts, requesting a lock of her deceased husband's *hair*, to be preserved in a *Golden Urn*, with the jewels and regalia of the Grand Lodge.

"In complying with this request by sending the lock of hair which you will find inclosed, Mrs. Washington begs me to assure you that she views with gratitude the tributes of respect and affection paid to the memory of her dear deceased husband; and receives with a feeling heart the expressions of sympathy contained in your letter.

With great respect and esteem, I have the honor to be, gentlemen, your most obedient servant,

"Tobias Lear.

"John Warren,
"Paul Revere,   } Past Grand Masters."
"Josiah Bartlett,

Agreeably to previous notice, upon the 11th of February, the Grand Lodge performed Masonic funeral ceremonies in honor of their illustrious brother. At eight o'clock in the morning the bells commenced tolling, and at eleven a grand procession, composed of upwards of sixteen hundred brethren, was formed at the Old State House, and moved in Masonic order. Each brother bore a sprig of acacia, and the Golden Urn that contained the lock of Washington's hair was borne by six distinguished brethren. Many appropriate devices and emblems decorated the procession, and it was probably the most imposing one the Fraternity had ever formed in America. It passed through several of the principal streets of Boston to the Old South Meeting House, where public solemnities were performed, with prayers, odes, dirges, and a eulogy by Dr. Timothy Bigelow. From the Old South Church the procession then moved to the Stone Chapel, where a funeral service was performed by the Rev. Brother Bentley, Grand Chaplain, assisted by the Rev. Brother Dr. Walter. Flowers were then strewn, the acacia deposited, and the brethren returned to the Old State House, where the procession had formed, and there separated. The Golden Urn, with its precious treasure was deposited in the archives of the Grand Lodge, where it has since remained.

St. John's Lodge, at Boston, the oldest Masonic daughter of England on this continent, held in its hall, one week previous to the above Grand Lodge proceedings, private funeral solemnities, at which a eulogy was delivered by Bro. George Blake. At a meeting of that lodge, held on the 26th of March, it was voted that a copy of that eulogy, handsomely bound, together with a *Golden Medal*, be transmitted to the Grand Lodge of England, accompanied with an address; and a committee was appointed to form the address and transmit these memorials to their mother Grand Lodge; but we have failed to find the evidence that it was carried into effect.

In New Hampshire, Masonic funeral honors to Washington were shown by most of the lodges in that State, by joining with the citizens at large, in testifying grief for his loss and respect for his memory. The New Hampshire Gazette of January 8, 1800, contains the following paragraph:

"The Grand Lodge of New Hampshire are unanimous in opinion, that to mourn with our fellow-citizens at large, would be more respectable to our late illustrious brother, and more honorable, than particular society lodges of mourning. The loss is deep and universal; so ought to be our testimonials of respect decent and uniform throughout the United States. But in our lodges will be the seat of sorrow."

Nathaniel Adams was at that time the Grand Master of Masons in New Hampshire, and in his "Annals of Portsmouth" he says:

"1799.—Tuesday, the 31st day of December, was set apart to commemorate the death of the illustrious Washington, who departed this life on the 14th of this month. At an early hour all public offices, stores, and shops were closed. Business and pleasure were suspended. At cloven o'clock a procession moved from the Assembly-room to St. John's Church, in the following order:

"The companies of Artillery, Light Infantry, and Governor Oilman's Blues, with muffled drums, music in crape, arms reversed, side-arms with black bows; martial music playing the Dead March in Saul; the Grand Lodge of New Hampshire, accompanied by St. John's Lodge, and many visiting brethren in the habiliments of their order; the orator and rector of St. John's Church; United States military officers; commissioned officers of the militia; select-men; clergy; citizens and strangers two and two.

"When the procession reached the church, a solemn piece of music was performed on the organ. Rev. Mr. Willard read the service of the church, and Jonathan Mewell Esq., pronounced an eulogy on the sorrowful occasion. A vast concourse of people attended, and almost every individual of respectability wore a crape as a badge of mourning, and all the shipping in the harbor hoisted their flags half-mast high."

Although the ceremonies on this occasion were not designed as Masonic, yet the ode which was sung was strictly so. It was composed by the Rev. Brother George Richards; and so highly did the brethren of St. John's Lodge appreciate it, that, at their next meeting, they voted that it be sung each lodge-night for the three following months, and that all other songs be excluded during that time.

The news of the death of Washington reached Bennington, Vermont, on the 25th of December. The court of the county was there in session, and upon the sad event being therein announced, it was adjourned for the day, and in the evening a large meeting was held, at which Isaac Tichneob, the governor of the State, presided; and it was determined that a public demonstration of sorrow should be made by a procession and suitable discourses on Friday the 27th.

At two o'clock on that day, a large number of citizens convened at the courthouse, and a procession was formed, in which the Masonic Fraternity occupied a conspicuous place. With muffled drums and music playing a solemn dirge, the procession moved to the church, where the Rev. Mr. Sweet delivered a discourse to the general audience, after which, Anthony Haswell delivered an oration in behalf of the Masonic brethren. The ceremonies at the church were closed by an ode prepared by Brother Haswell for the occasion. The procession then returned to the courthouse, where the Fraternity partook of a repast prepared for them. By recommendation of the Grand Master of Vermont, the brethren there wore a badge of mourning for Washington six months.

In Rhode Island, also, the principal demonstrations of sorrow for the death of Washington, were in conjunction with the public ceremonies of all classes of citizens in that State. As soon as his death became known, the Grand Master of Masons in that jurisdiction issued the following order:

"By order of the Most Worshipful Peleg Clark, Grand Master of the State of Rhode Island.

"All brethren under the jurisdiction of this Grand Lodge, are required to wear a black scarf on the left arm for nine days, as a token of regard for the loss of our late illustrious Brother George Washington.
"By order,
"John Handy, G. Secretary.
"NEWPORT, December 23, 1799."

The records of the subordinate lodges, both in Rhode Island and Connecticut, show that a general mourning was adopted on the sad event; and that in all the numerous public processions and ceremonies, the Fraternity were assigned a post of dignity, in consideration of the well-known connection Washington had with their Society. It is impossible in this sketch to give even a synopsis of the rich treasures such records in the various States contain, relating to funeral ceremonies on that occasion. They are worthy of a volume. From our portfolio of these rich memorials of merited regard, we will select but one other. It is the mourning of the brethren at Fredericksburg, where Washington had been made a Mason nearly fifty years before. Youthful craftsmen had in those long years taken the places of most of the ancient brethren of that lodge; but there were some who still remembered, how, when youth and manhood were mingling their lines upon his brow, he sought their altar and bound himself to them in vows of brotherhood. These unbroken vows had been kept in their memory. There was now sadness in their hearts when they were summoned by their Master to meet and commemorate his loss. It was the second Sabbath after his death, and amidst the tolling of bells, which had commenced at sunrise, they met in their lodge-room at ten o'clock. The Grand Master of Virginia, Major Benjamin Day, was with them, and having taken the chair in the East, he thus addressed the lodge:

"We are now, brethren, to pay the last tribute of affection and respect to the eminent virtues and exemplary conduct that adorned the character of our worthy deceased Brother, George Washington. He was early initiated in this venerable lodge, as I am respectably informed, in the mysteries of our ancient and honorable profession; and having held it in the highest and most just veneration, the fraternal attention we now show to his memory is the more incumbent on us. He is gone forever from our view; but gone to the realms of celestial bliss, where the shafts of malice and detraction cannot penetrate, where all sublunary distinctions cease, and merit is rewarded by the scale of unerring justice. While the tear of sympathy is excited for a loss so generally and deservedly lamented, let us recollect that posterity will not less justly appreciate the talents and virtues he possessed. As a man, he was frail; and it would be a compliment to which human nature cannot aspire to suppose him free from peculiarities, or exempt from error. But let those that best know him determine the measure to which they extend. In the offices of private life, he was most endeared to those who were most in his familiarity and intimacy. In the various important appointments of public confidence. let not the sin of ingratitude sully the historic page, by denying him the incense of public applause. Abler Panegyrists will attend at the sacred altar, and do that justice to his memory to which his merits entitle him; while attendant angels await his immortal spirit in the mansions of eternal peace.

"Suffer me, brethren, on this solemn occasion, to remind you of the instability of all human concerns, and the un- certainty of our continuance in this transitory state of our existence. Let the example of our worthy deceased brother, and the amiable precepts of our institution, guide us in our conduct to each other; and the sacred volume, always open for our instruction in our duty to the inconceivably great, omnipotent, and merciful Architect of the Universe! That when it shall please Him to relieve us from the cares and solicitude of this probationary state, we may not be dismayed, but with a well-grounded hope, familiarized to the expectation of a change, the awful, yet the inevitable lot of mortality, and the entrance into a lodge of perfect harmony and eternal happiness."

The lodge then formed a procession, and moved from their hall, preceded by music playing a solemn dirge, to the public parade-ground, where they were received by the military with reversed arms, who escorted them to the church, where a discourse was delivered by the Rev. Mr. Stephenson, from the words: "*And the Lord spake unto Joshua, the son of Nun,*

Moses' minister, saying, Moses my servant is dead." The solemnities of the day were concluded by the military firing sixteen minute-guns as the brethren returned to their lodge-room.

The official inventory of Washington's estate after his death was duly entered in the records of Fairfax County, and from it we are able to show that he treasured in his cabinet and in his library, to the close of his life, the Masonic souvenirs he had at various times received from his brethren, thus verifying also our records and traditions of his reception of them. The statements which we have given in the foregoing sketch, embrace his reception of Masonic regalia from Messrs. Watson & Cassoul; a box containing a Masonic apron and sash from La Fayette; the Pennsylvania Ahiman Rezon from the Grand Lodge of Pennsylvania; the Book of Constitutions of the Grand Lodge of Massachusetts, from that Grand Lodge; "Proofs of a Conspiracy," from the Rev. Mr. Snyder; and an Ahiman Rezon, or Book of Constitutions, from the Grand Lodge of Maryland. All of the above books we find inventoried by the appraisers of his personal estate, as follows: The Pennsylvania Ahiman Eezon, one dollar; the Massachusetts Grand Lodge Constitution, one dollar; "Proofs of a Conspiracy," one dollar and fifty cents; Maryland Ahiman Eezon, one dollar and fifty cents.

We also find in the same inventory, a volume of Masonic Sermons, fifty cents. The same list also contains a "Japan box containing a Mason's apron," inventoried at fifty dollars; and a "Piece of oil-cloth containing Orders of Masonry," fifty dollars. The first of these was probably the box and apron sent by La Fayette, the term Japan referring to the fine exterior polish of the box. The last was doubtless what is called the Masoris carpet or floor-dotli. We have never met with any other mention of this last Masonic relic of

Washington's, except in this official inventory, and are at loss to know when it came into his possession, and what finally became of it. So interesting and valuable a relic of Washington should not be lost; and we here request that if its history or existence be known, it be communicated to the Fraternity of which our illustrious brother was the pride and ornament.

Reader, we have sketched for you Washington as a Mason. Learn from it, that

> "Ere mature manhood marked his youthful brow,
> He sought our altar and he made his vow
> Upon our tesselated floor he trod,
> Bended his knees, and placed his trust in God!
> Through all his great and glorious life he stood
> A true, warm brother, foremost e'er in good;
> And when he died, amid a nation's gloom,
> His mourning brethren bore him to the tomb!"

Laying of the Cornerstone of the Washington Monument

The proposed park would contain about fifty-two acres, which it was designed "to fence in and lay out in drives, walks, and trees, and to erect thereon a National Monument in the center thereof." The position would command a view of all the public buildings, particularly from the Monument, "which is to be one hundred and fifty feet high," and "devoted to the public as a place of resort where busts, statues, and paintings of all the great men connected with the history of our country may be seen. The site is nearly opposite to the Patent and Post Office buildings, or center of the city, and but a square or two south of the great thoroughfare of the city, the Pennsylvania avenue, which, in point of magnitude and of easy approach to our citizens, there is no ground in the

District, or in any other country, which could vie with it as a public square of beauty and recreation."

Lots were to be sold at auction and proceeds used for creating the park, as described in the resolution, and "so that preparations may be immediately made" for a "site for a National Monument, which in the course of a few years will become a beautiful resort for the citizens and visitors of the District as well as for strangers from all parts of the world." The park would have circles and every device of walk, all the emblems of the Nation together with forest trees of every State, plants, flowers, &c. The construction of a national monument the committee regarded as of great interest to the American people. Half a century had passed away, and no worthy memorial is found in the Capital. The committee recommend the "temple form" as best for a monument, "built to contain busts and statues of Presidents and other illustrious men of the country, as well as 'paintings' of historical subjects." The construction of the Monument "would carry out the views of this Society to erect a monument to Washington," and which it is understood will apply its funds toward this object "whenever Congress shall authorize its erection on some portion of the public ground," the site to be due west of the Capitol. The construction was to be under the direction of the President of the United States and the Washington Monument Society. A plan of the proposed temple form of monument accompanied the report, a statue of Washington surmounting its dome.

While the Society at this time was willing to concede a change in the form of the Monument, and apply funds collected to speedily realize such change, no action by Congress resulted from the report quoted so far as authorizing the building of the National Monument suggested by the committee or lending aid to the Society, or granting a site for the Monument it had projected.

In 1845 the Society removed generally the limitation of one dollar as the amount of a subscription. This action seems to have been wise, as the later annual gross receipts were for a time greatly increased.

In view of the previous recognition by the Society of this evil of limitation of contributions, it is surprising that it was not generally removed when it was specially removed for the occasion of the census in 1840.

In 1846 the Society issued a further address "to the American people," announcing that it had "appointed the Hon. Elisha Whittlesey, of Ohio, the General Agent of the Society, whose office will be held in Washington. To him has been delegated the power of appointing subagents, who will receive a commission on the funds they may collect as a compensation for their services. * * * It is scarcely necessary to remark that the character of the General Agent appointed by the Board of Managers to make additional collections for the Monument is such as to insure success and produce entire confidence. It is known to the whole country; and Mr. Whittlesey's efforts in this new and noble undertaking, it is hoped, will be crowned with that success which cannot fail to accompany so glorious an object. It was further said by this address:

"It may be proper to state for the information of the public that the delay in commencing the Monument has been occasioned by the want of a proper site, which the Board had hoped would long since have been granted by Congress. * * * The Board designed at an early period to commence the Monument, but as no site could be obtained sufficiently eligible on any other ground than the public mall, near the Potomac, and as that could only be obtained by a grant from Congress, which has not yet been made, that purpose has been unavoidably postponed until the next session of the National Legislature, when it is believed no objection will be made to allow the Board the use of "the ground it desires for so laudable and patriotic an object."

This address, signed by the officers of the Society, James K. Polk, ex officio President; Wm. Brent, First Vice-President; Mayor of Washington, Third Vice-President; J. B. H. Smith, Treasurer; George Watterston, Secretary; and by the entire Board of Managers, including among the number Maj. Gen. Winfield Scott, Thos. Carbery, Peter Force, Philip R. Fendall, Gen. Nathan Townson, Gen. Walter Jones, Col. J. Kearney, J. J. Abert, W. A. Bradley, and Thomas Munroe, contained the following eloquent language:

"The pilgrim to Mount Vernon, the spot consecrated by Washington's hallowed remains, is often shocked when he looks upon the humble sepulchre which contains his dust, and laments that no monument has yet reared its lofty head to mark a Nation's gratitude.

"It is true that the storied urn, the animated bust, or the splendid mausoleum, cannot call back the departed spirit, or ' soothe the dull, cold ear of death;' but it is equally true that it can and does manifest the gratitude and veneration of the living for those who have passed away forever from the stage of life and left behind them the cherished memory of their virtues. The posthumous honors bestowed by a grateful nation on its distinguished citizens serve the further purpose of stimulating those who survive them to similar acts of greatness and of virtue, while the respect and admiration of the country which confers them upon its children are more deeply and ardently felt. The character of Washington is identified with the glory and greatness of his country. It belongs to history, into which it has infused a moral grandeur and beauty.

"It presents a verdant oasis on the dreary waste of the world, on which the mind loves to repose, and the patriot and philosopher delights to dwell. Such a being but seldom appears to illustrate and give splendor to the annals of mankind, and the country which gave him birth should take a pride in bestowing posthumous honors on his name. It is not to transmit the name or fame of the illustrious Washington to future ages that a Monument should be erected to his memory ; but to show that the People of this Republic at least are not ungrateful, and that they desire to manifest their love of eminent public and private virtues by some enduring memorial which, like the pyramids of Egypt, shall fatigue time by its duration."

The General Agent, Mr. Whittlesey, submitted a plan which was adopted by the Society for a systematic collection of funds, which included constituting Congressional districts as distinct collection districts, and in 1847 a circular letter was addressed to Members of Congress respecting the formation of such districts and the appointment of collecting agents therein. As formerly, it was required that the appointee should be well recommended and endorsed by Representatives, Senators, and well-known citizens of the district or State. It was also determined to specially appeal to the Masonic fraternity of the country.

The agents appointed were supplied with properly prepared blank books for the autograph enrollment of contributors, which books, when filled with names, were to be returned to the office of the Society for deposit and safe keeping.

On the request of the Society, Mrs. James Madison, Mrs. John Quincy Adams, and Mrs. Alexander

Hamilton effected an organization of ladies to aid in collecting funds for the proposed Monument. Through appeals, entertainments, fairs, and many social functions given for the purpose by ladies in various parts of the country, there resulted but a very moderate addition to the funds of the Society, but in no way commensurate with its expectations in the premises.

On the 29th of February, 1847, the Society adopted the following resolution offered by Mr. Brent:

"Resolved, That the several Consuls of the United States abroad, and the Pursers of the Navy, be requested by the General Agent to solicit subscriptions for the erection of a suitable National Monument to the memory of Washington from American citizens, seamen, and others of liberal patriotic feelings, and that the Secretary of State and the Secretary of the Navy be respectfully requested, on behalf of the National Washington Monument Society, to cause to be forwarded the letters and papers necessary to accomplish the object embraced in this resolution."

In accordance with this resolve (the consent of the Honorable Secretary of State and the Honorable Secretary of the Navy having been given), a circular letter was prepared and sent out to the persons named in the resolution.

After setting forth the object of the Society, and earnestly appealing for funds to accomplish that purpose, the circular stated a compensation of 20 percent, would be allowed on funds collected and faithfully accounted for. This circular was accompanied by a supply of "prints," to be distributed to subscribers, as follows:

"Copies of a large portrait of Washington, copied from Stuart's painting in Faneuil Hall, Boston. Copies of the large print of the design of the Monument.

Smaller prints of the same subjects were also furnished."

The subscriber of $5.00 was to receive one of the large prints; of $8.00, both the large prints; of $1.00, one of the small prints ; and to the subscriber of $1.50, both of the small prints. It was also publicly announced that the cornerstone of the Monument would be laid "on the 4th of July next, and arrangements will be made to give to the ceremony a national character corresponding with the character and magnitude of the work."

The accounts of the Treasurer of the Society from time to time show, in response to this special appeal, a considerable collection of funds, especially among the officers and seamen of the Navy.

In 1847, the aggregate of collections and accumulated interest was some $87,000, which amount was deemed sufficient to justify the Society in beginning the erection of the Monument. A resolution was adopted that the cornerstone be laid on the 22d of February next "provided that a suitable site can be obtained in time," and a committee was appointed to apply to Congress early in the session for a "site on the public mall for the Monument." A committee was also appointed to ascertain "the best terms on which a suitable site on private grounds within the limits of the City of Washington can be obtained."

Before the latter committee reported, in response to the memorial by the Society to Congress, desiring action by that body to accord a site for the Monument, on the 31st of January, 1848, Congress passed a resolution authorizing the Washington National Monument Society to erect "a Monument to the memory of George Washington upon such portion of the public grounds or reservations within the City of Washington, not otherwise occupied, as shall be selected by the President of the United States and the

Board of Managers of said Society as a suitable site on which to erect the said Monument, and for the necessary protection thereof."

January 25, 1848, General Archibald Henderson, Lieut. M. F. Maury, and Mr. Walter Lenox were appointed a committee to make the necessary arrangements to lay the cornerstone, but it being found impossible to make arrangements for that ceremony on the 22d of February, on the 29th of January it was postponed until July 4th following.

SITE OF THE MONUMENT.

The site selected under the authority of the resolution of Congress was the public reservation, numbered 3, on the plan of the City of Washington, containing upwards of thirty acres, where the Monument now stands, near the Potomac river, west of the Capitol and south of the President's House. The deed was executed on the 12th day of April, 1849, and was duly recorded among the land records of the District of Columbia on the 22d day of February, 1849.

This deed was executed by James K. Polk, President of the United States, "and in testimony of the selection as aforesaid of the said reservation, numbered three (3), for the purpose aforesaid," was also signed by William Brent, First Vice-President; W. W. Seaton, Second Vice-President; Archibald Henderson, Third Vice-President; J. B. H. Smith, Treasurer; George Watterston, Secretary; and Peter Force; the signing being "in the presence of Winfield Scott, Nathan Towson, John. J. Abert, Walter Jones, Thomas Carbery, W. A. Bradley, P. R. Fendall, Thomas Munroe, Walter Lenox, M. F. Maury, Thomas Blagden."

As to the reasons for the selection of this particular site, we find them stated by the Society in an address to the country, in later years, as follows:

"The site selected presents a beautiful view of the Potomac; is so elevated that the Monument will be seen from all parts of the city and the surrounding country, and, being a public reservation, it is safe from any future obstruction of the view.

"It is so near the river that materials for constructing the Monument can be conveyed to it from the river at but little expense ; stone, sand, and lime, all of the best kind, can be brought to it by water from convenient distances; and marble of the most beautiful quality, obtained at a distance of only eleven miles from Baltimore, on the Susquehanna railroad, can be brought either on the railroad or in vessels. In addition to these and kindred reasons, the adoption of the site was further and impressively recommended by the consideration that the Monument to be erected on it would be in full view of Mount Vernon, where rest the ashes of the Chief; and by evidence that Washington himself, whose unerring judgment had selected this city to be the Capital of the Nation, had also selected this particular spot for a Monument to the American Revolution, which in the year 1795 it was proposed should be erected or placed at the 'permanent seat of Government of the United States.'

This Monument was to have been executed by Ceracchi, a Roman sculptor, and paid for by contributions of individuals. The same site is marked on Major L'Enfant's map of Washington City for the equestrian statue of General Washington, ordered by Congress in 1783, which map was examined, approved, and transmitted to Congress by him when President of the United States."

It may be here remarked, with reference to the site selected for the Monument, that the foundations were laid but a short distance to the east of the meridian line, run, at the instance of President Jefferson, by

Nicholas King, surveyor, October 15, 1804. The report of Mr. King, as found in the Department of State, bears the endorsement, "to be filed in the office of State as a record of demarcation of the first meridian of the United States." This line, by the President's instructions, passed through the center of the White House, and where it intersected a line due east and west through the center of the Capitol a small monument or pyramid of stones was placed—an object which disappeared about the year 1874, in the process of improving the Monument grounds. It would also appear that the center of the District of Columbia, within its original lines, was not far removed northwestward from the Monument as it stands, being near the corner of Seventeenth and C streets, N.W., 1,305 feet north and 1,579 feet west of the Monument. (*National Geographic Magazine*, vol. 6, p. 149.)

It does not appear, however, that these latter existing facts were in any manner considered by the Board of Managers in the selection of the site for the Monument. The cornerstone for the Monument, a block of marble weighing "twenty-four thousand five hundred pounds," was quarried and presented to the Society by Mr. Thomas Symington, of Baltimore, Md. On its arrival in the city, the stone was enthusiastically drawn to the site of the Monument by many workmen from the navy yard, and other persons.

In planning the ceremonies to occur on the laying of the cornerstone of the Monument, the Society invited ex-President John Quincy Adams to deliver the oration, but the invitation, however, was regretfully declined by Mr. Adams on account of the state of his health. Hon. Daniel Webster being requested to deliver the oration declined because of pressure of business and the shortness of the time allowed in which to prepare one. Honorable Robert C. Winthrop, of Massachusetts, the Speaker of the House of

Representatives, being then requested consented to deliver the oration.

Invitations were sent by the committee of arrangements to Mrs. Alexander Hamilton, Mrs. Dolly P. Madison, Mrs. John Quincy Adams, Martin Van Buren, Millard Fillmore, Lewis Cass, General Sam Houston, Chief Justice Taney, George Washington Parke Custis, and other distinguished persons to attend the ceremonies of the laying of the cornerstone.

The replies received indicate the interest of those invited in the erection of the Monument to Washington. For the occasion transportation lines entering the District of Columbia reduced their usual rates of travel.

On the 4th of July, 1848, under a bright sky, in the presence of the President and Vice-President of the United States, Senators and Representatives in Congress, Heads of Executive Departments, and other officers of the Government, the Judiciary, Representatives of Foreign Governments, the corporate authorities of Washington, Georgetown, and Alexandria, military commands, associations of many descriptions, delegations from States and Territories and from several Indian tribes, and a great multitude of citizens, the cornerstone was laid.

The Rev. Mr. McJilton offered the consecration prayer, and the oration, lofty and eloquent, was delivered by the Hon. Robert C. Winthrop. Mr. Benj. B. French, Grand Master of the Masonic Fraternity of the United States, then delivered a beautiful and appropriate address, after which he descended to the corner-stone and performed the Masonic ceremonies of laying it.

The gavel used was that employed by George Washington, as Master Mason, in the Masonic ceremonies in the laying of the corner-stone of the National Capitol. A patriotic song, written by Robert

Treat Paine, was sung, after which the benediction was pronounced.

The corner-stone was laid at the northeast angle of the foundation. Among the distinguished guests on the stand at the laying of the cornerstone were Mrs. Alexander Hamilton (then ninety-one years old), Mrs. Dolly Paine Madison, George Washington Parke Custis, and others of eminence. The proceedings are thus discussed in the papers
of the times : ******

"The day was fine. The rain had laid the dust and infused a delicious freshness in the air. The procession was extensive and beautiful. It embraced many military companies of our own and our sister cities—various associations, with their characteristic emblems; the President arid Cabinet and various officers of the Executive Departments; many of the Members of Congress; citizens and strangers who had poured into the city. When the lengthened procession had reached the site of the Monument they were joined by a whole cortege of ladies and gentlemen ; and we are free to say we never beheld so magnificent a spectacle. From 15,000 to 20,000 persons, are estimated to have been present, stretched over a large area of ground from the southern hill, gradually sloping down to the plain below.

General Lafayette

"In a hollow spread with boards and surrounded with seats the crowd gathered. Around two sides of this space were high and solidly-constructed seats, hired out to spectators, covered with awnings, and affording a favorable position for seeing and hearing. A temporary arch was erected, covered with colored cotton and suitably embellished. But its most attractive ornament was a living American eagle, with its dark plumage, piercing eye, and snowy head and tail, who seemed to look with anxious gaze on the unwonted spectacle below. This is the same eagle which in Alexandria surmounted the arch of welcome there erected to Lafayette; and to complete its honors and its public character, it has since been entrusted to M. Vattemare, to be presented to the National Museum in Paris. He is now forty years old.

"The fireworks (at night) exhibited on the same theatre, and prepared by the pyrotechnists of the navy yard, were admirable beyond description. They were witnessed by an immense multitude. The President's reception at night in the East Room was very numerously attended. Thus passed one of the most splendid and agreeable days Washington has ever witnessed."

Objections having been from time to time urged against the plan of the Monument, the Society, early in 1848, appointed a committee to consider them. In April of that year, pursuant to a report of a committee of its members, the Society fixed upon a height of 500 feet for the shaft, leaving in abeyance the surrounding pantheon and base. And this modification continued to be the plan of the Monument until it was again altered at a later period. The cornerstone laid, the Society began active operations to raise the shaft, which were most vigorously prosecuted. The purchase of materials and the general construction of the Monument, embracing the employment of labor, skilled and common, were committed by the Society to three of their number, denominated a Building Committee. The members of this committee devoted much of their time patriotically to the duties assigned them, held weekly meetings during several years, and served without any sort of compensation
whatever.

July 17, 1849, was commenced the movement to procure a memorial stone for the Washington Monument, and this was accomplished by subscription and the stone placed in the following year. It is located on the third landing, or first stop, of the elevator, and is of white granulated marble. Its face is six feet by two feet three inches, and bears the inscription "Grand Lodge of the District of Columbia.

Our Brother, George Washington." In the center of the inscription are the square and compasses, all in raised work, and within and protected by a heavy molding. In an aperture of the block there were placed a list of the contributors and the last printed proceedings of the Grand Lodge. "Thus," in the language of Grand Master French, "have the Freemasons of this jurisdiction presented their offering at the holy shrine of patriotism."

DEDICATION OF THE MONUMENT IN 1885

By far the most important event of the year 1885, or, indeed, of many years, in local Masonry was the participation of the Fraternity in the dedication of the Washington Monument. This great work, which had halted early in its career, owes its final completion largely to the efforts of the Masonic brethren of this and other jurisdictions, who, through the long period of inaction, persistently worked toward that end. The preparations for the event gave rise to a situation which led to the reiteration by the then Grand Master, M. W. Bro. M. M. Parker, of the principle adhered to for some years and previously mentioned, that the Fraternity might not take part in any public function in which no Masonic work was required of it. The story, in brief, follows: The first invitation extended by the Joint Congressional Commission on Dedication assigned to the Masons a prominent and distinctive part in the ceremony and was satisfactory. Later, however, the Commission decided to curtail the ceremony to one oration, but offered to give the Fraternity "a position of honor in the line." Grand Master Parker replied that "the practice of Masonry was not to swell processions," and declined to invite the Grand Lodge, and, altho importuned by prominent officials, continued to reaffirm that "under no circumstances could the Grand Lodge be induced to depart from its ancient customs."

Grand Master M. M. Parker

At a later date the Joint Commission invited the Grand Master to meet with it, when the matter was thoroughly gone over, with the result that an invitation was received and accepted by the Grand Lodge to take part in the ceremonies and active steps were at once taken to make the occasion a notable one. Circular letters were sent to all the Grand Lodges of the United States and those foreign grand bodies with which we were in fraternal correspondence and suitable arrangements made for Knights Templar escort and entertainment.

On the date set, February 21, 1885, the Grand Lodge met in special session in the main hall of the Temple, with an unusual number of brethren in attendance, including representatives from the Grand Lodges of Massachusetts, Pennsylvania, New York, Delaware, North Carolina, Virginia, New Hampshire, California, Tennessee, Maryland, West Virginia. and Illinois.

Escorted by the Knights Templar and Royal Arch Masons of the District, lodges from Delaware, Virginia, and New York, and delegations in force from each of the lodges of this jurisdiction, the Grand Lodge proceeded to the Monument in orderly Masonic formation, where, after an invocation by Rev. Mr. Suter and an address by the late W. W. Corcoran, the full Masonic ceremony of dedication was performed according to usage.

Following this ceremony Grand Master Parker delivered a striking eulogy upon the life and character of the illustrious Washington, in the course of which he took occasion to refer to and display the following interesting relics: The gavel used by Washington at the laying of the cornerstone of the Capitol; the Bible, belonging to Fredericksburg Lodge, No. 4, of Virginia, upon which he took his first Masonic vows; the Bible, belonging to St. John's Lodge, No. 1, of New York, upon which he took the oath of office as the first President of the United States; the Great Light, belonging to Alexandria-Washington Lodge, No. 22, of Alexandria, Va., upon which he, as Master of that lodge, received the vows of initiates; the apron worn by him, which was wrought by Madame LaFayette; a lock of his hair, presented by Mrs. Washington to the Grand Lodge of Massachusetts and encased in a golden urn, the gift of the late Bro. Paul Revere, and a candle, one of the Lesser Lights used at the funeral exercises at Mt. Vernon in 1799.

Laying of the Cornerstone of Washington D.C.

Behold, I lay in Zion for a foundation a stone, a tried stone, a precious corner-stone, a sure foundation."
—Isaiah xxviii, 16.

That freemasonry was a dominating tho unobtrusive force from the very first in this section has striking illustration in the fact that the cornerstone of the District was laid with Masonic ceremonies, and this event, probably without a parallel in the world's annals, furnishes, perhaps, the most natural, certainly the most interesting, point of departure in the historical journey we are about to undertake.

The word cornerstone is here used in no figurative sense, but refers to a small marker of masonry set up at Jones Point, on Hunting Creek, below Alexandria, Va., from which were run at right angles the lines which formed the first two sides of the ten-mile square constituting the original District of Columbia. This initial stone was placed according to ancient Masonic usages, April 15, 1791, by the Masonic Lodge of Alexandria, Va., which had been chartered eight years before by the Grand Lodge of Pennsylvania as No. 39, and which, in 1788, became Alexandria-Washington Lodge, No. 22, under the jurisdiction of Virginia, with George Washington as Master. This lodge, with one chartered in Georgetown as No. 9, of Maryland, in 1789, constituted organized Masonry within the limits of the contemplated new Territory, and while there remains to us only the most meager account of this first public recorded Masonic function yet it may be surmised that the latter lodge was also in evidence on that eventful Spring day and took an active part in the exercises.

The following account of the affair, published at the time in a Philadelphia paper, is deemed worthy of reproduction:

ALEXANDRIA, April 21, 1791.
On Friday, the 15th inst., the Hon. Daniel Carroll and Hon. David Stuart arrived in this town to superintend the fixing of the first cornerstone of the Federal District. The Mayor and the Commonalty, together with the members of the different Lodges of the town, at three o'clock, waited on the commissioners at Mr. Wise's, where they dined, and, after drinking a glass of wine to the following sentiment, viz.:

"May the stone which we are about to place in the ground, remain an immovable monument of the wisdom and unanimity of North America," the company proceeded to Jones Point in the following order:

1st. The Town Sergeant.
2d. Hon. Daniel Carroll and the Mayor.
3d. Mr. Ellicott and the Recorder.
4th. Such of the Common Council and Aldermen as were not Freemasons.
5th. Strangers.
6th. The Master of Lodge, No. 22, with Dr. David Stuart on his right, and the Rev. James Muir [for many years an active Mason] on his left, followed by the rest of the Fraternity, in their usual form of procession.
Lastly. The citizens, two by two.

When Mr. Ellicott had ascertained the precise point from which the first line of the District was to proceed, the Master of the Lodge and Dr. Steuart, assisted by others of their brethren, placed the stone. After which a deposit of corn, wine, and oil was placed upon it, and the following observations were made by the Rev. James Muir:

"Of America it may be said, as of Judea of old, that it is a good land and large—a land of brooks of waters, of fountains, and depths that spring out of the valleys and hills—a land of wheat, and barley, and vines, and fig-trees, and pomegranates—a land of oil, olives, and honey—a land wherein we eat bread without scarceness, and have lack of nothing—a land whose stones are iron, and out of whose hills thou mayst dig brass— a land which the Lord thy God careth for;—the eyes of the Lord thy God are always upon it; from the beginning of the year even unto the end of the year.

"May Americans be grateful and virtuous, and they shall insure the indulgence of Providence; may they be unanimous and just, and they shall rise to greatness. May true patriotism actuate every heart; may it be the devout and universal wish. Peace be within thy walls, O America, and prosperity within thy palaces! Amiable it is for brethren to dwell together in unity; it is more fragrant than the perfumes on Aaron's garment; it is more refreshing than the dews on Hermon's hill.

"May this stone long commemorate the goodness of God in those uncommon events which have given America a name among nations. Under this stone may jealousy and selfishness be forever buried. From this stone may a superstructure arise, whose glory, whose magnificence, whose stability, unequalled hitherto, shall astonish the world, and invite even the savage of the wilderness to take shelter under its roof."

The company partook of some refreshments, and then returned to the place from whence they came, where a number of toasts were drank; and the following was delivered by the Master of the Lodge (Dr. Dick), and was received with every token of approbation:

"Brethren and Gentlemen: May jealousy, that green-eyed monster, be buried deep under the work which we have this day completed, never to rise again within the Federal District."

The lighthouse structure now on Jones Point covers the site of these interesting ceremonies.

Paul Revere

Saint Andrew's Lodge of Free Masons was organized November 30, 1756, by the Grand Lodge of Scotland. Its charter was not received until September 4, 1760, when it was laid before the Lodge, and in the same evening work was commenced under it by receiving Paul Revere, a goldsmith and engraver as an Entered Apprentice.

The *Boston Post Boy*, two years later, contained the following:

"Notice is hereby given to the Brethren of the Ancient and Honorable Society of Free and Accepted Mason, That the Feast of St. John the Baptist will be celebrated by the Brethren of St. Andrew's Lodge, (duly authoriz'd, constituted and appointed to be held at Boston, by the Right Honorable, Lord Aberdour, grand Master of Scotland) on Thursday the 24th Instant, at

the Royal Exchange Tavern in King Street. Tickets to be had of,
"Joseph Webb, Jun.
"Phillip Lewis,
"Paul Revere.
   "Boston, June 14, 1762."

In 1769 Revere became the Secretary of this Lodge, and from 1770 to 1771 was its Master,—succeeding Joseph Warren,—as also from 1777 to 1779, and 1780 to 1782.

Exchange Coffee House

The Exchange Coffee House, which was situated on Congress Square with entrance on State (King) and Devonshire (Pudding Lane) Streets. A number of Masonic Lodges met in its upper stories. It was burned November 3, 1818.

Green Dragon Tavern

The "Massachusetts Grand Lodge" was organized at Mason's Hall in the Green Dragon Tavern, December 27, 1769, by its first Grand Master, Joseph Warren, who was commissioned May 30, 1769, by the Grand Master of Masons in Scotland — Rt. Hon. George, Earl of Dalhousie, — "to be Grand Master of Masons in Boston, New England, and within one hundred miles of the same."

Sign of the Green Dragon Tavern

Revere was made its "Senior Grand Deacon;" and he was one of the committee with Warren to apply to the Scottish Masons for this charter. September 19 of this year, St. Andrew's Lodge voted: "That the Lodge adhere to old regulations: that the G. Lodge be provided with Jewels made of any metal under silver: that the Lodge accept Bro. Paul Revere's offer to make the Jewels, and wait for his pay, till the G. Lodge is in cash."

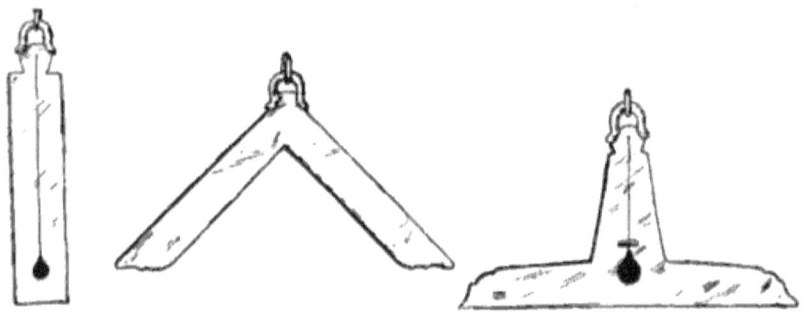

Silver Masonic Jewels Fashioned by Paul Revere

After the re-interment of Gen. Joseph Warren in the Granary Burial Ground, the Grand Lodge having returned to the State House, the following vote was passed:

"COUNCIL CHAMBER, Boston, April 8, 1776."

"At a meeting of the Grand Lodge, and a numerous body of Free and Accepted Masons, after the re-interment of our Most Worshipful Grand Master, Joseph Warren, Esq., who was slain in the battle of Bunker Hill, June 17, 1775.
"In the chair the Right Worshipful Joseph Webb, D. G. M. Voted, That our Brothers, Paul Revere, Edward Proctor, and Stephen Bruce, be a committee to wait on our Brother Perez Morton, Esq., and present our cordial thanks for his oration delivered this afternoon, and request a copy thereof for the press.
"Attest, William Hoskins, Grand Secretary."

In 1783, the question of allegiance arose in St. Andrew's Lodge; whether it should pass under the jurisdiction of the Massachusetts Grand Lodge, or remain by the Grand Lodge of Scotland. Twenty-nine members were for remaining and twenty-three against. This minority, under the lead of Revere, withdrew from St. Andrew's Lodge, and on the 4th of September, 1784, organized the "Rising States Lodge," which was chartered by the Massachusetts Grand Lodge, with Paul Revere as its first Master; his son Paul, Jr., joined this Lodge and became one of its officers. In the archives of the "New England Historic Genealogical Society" there is a handsome diploma of membership of this Lodge, engrossed on parchment, issued November 16, 1787, to James Henry Langier de Tassy, dully signed by Paul Revere, Master, and Paul Revere, Jr., Junior Warden. Mr. Langier was of the firm of Langier & Minot, Merchants, 36 State Street, Boston, and his residence was on Winter Street.

Boston's State Street - 1801

In 1785, there arose a question in the history of Masonry, as to the legality of the Massachusetts Grand Lodge, and a convention was held in Charlestown May 26, whereat delegates from twelve different Lodges met to consider and settle the matter. "Rt. Worshipful Paul Revere" was the first named in the list of delegates. Not until 1792, were all of these differences of opinion settled, when a "union took place between the St. John's and Massachusetts Grand Lodge, and it was ever after called The Grand Lodge of Massachusetts."

On the celebration of the "Festival of St. John, the Evangelist," June 24, 1791, the Rev. Dr. William Bentley, of Salem, delivered the address, which was afterwards printed, as were others of his Masonic discourses.

The following letter was sent to Mr. Bentley:

"Boston, June 27, 1791.
"REVEREND BROTHER BENTLEY.

"The unanimous voice of the Massachusetts Grand Lodge, through us their committee, tender you their cordial and brotherly thanks for your ingenious and well adapted discourse at the chapel on Friday last; and at the same time entreat the favour of a copy thereof for the press, which we flatter ourselves we shall receive from you.
"Your sudden departure from town deprived us of the honour we promised ourselves of waiting upon you personally.
"With the most affectionate salutation we are
"Very Respectfully
"Dear Brother
"Yours Affectionately
"M. M. Hayes,
"Paul Revere,
"Perez Morton,
"Josiah Bartlett."

Revere was Grand Master of the Grand Lodge of Massachusetts from 1794 to 1797. While in that position he wrote the "Charges" for installation of officers, still in use by the Masonic Fraternity. Some of the excellent sentiments therein are as follows: "Let complacency and benevolence flourish among you;" "May your love be reciprocal and harmonious;" "Avoid partiality, giving praise where it is due;" "You must preserve union, and judge in all cause amicably and mildly, preferring peace." He also presented to the "Massachusetts Historical Society," July 26 1796, in behalf of the Grand Lodge, "The Constitution of the Free and Accepted Masons," very elegantly bound.

Laying of the Boston, Massachusetts State House Cornerstone

The cornerstone of the present State House on Beacon Hill, Boston, was laid on the 4th of July, 1795. The State Government requested the Free Masons to take part in the ceremonies; and the officers and members of the different Masonic Lodges met with the State officers in Representative Hall, in the "Old State House," and thence proceeded, in Masonic order, to the "Old South Meeting House," where they listened to an oration by George Blake, Esq.; after which the procession was re-formed, and with the corner-stone, which was "on a truck, decorated with ribbons, drawn by 15 white horses – one for each state then in the Union, each with a leader," and escorted by the Independent Fusiliers, proceeded to the site.

Old Boston State House (West End)

When the stone was in position, duly squared, plumbed and leveled, His Excellency, Governor Samuel Adams, delivered the following address to the immense concourse of people there assembled:

"Fellow Citizens.

"The Representatives of the people in General Court assembled, did solemnly Resolve, that an Edifice be erected, upon this spot of ground for the purpose of holding the Public Councils of the Commonwealth of Massachusetts. By the request of their Agents and Commissioners, I do now lay the Corner-Stone. May the Superstructure be raised even to the top Stone without any untoward accident, and remain permanent as the everlasting mountains. May the principles of our excellent Constitution, founded in nature and in the Rights of Man, be ably defended here: and may the same principles be deeply engraven on the hearts of all citizens, and there be fixed, unimpaired, in full vigor, till time shall be no more."

Grand Master Revere then delivered the following address:

"Worshipful Brethren. I congratulate you on this auspicious day:--When the Arts and Sciences are establishing themselves in our happy country, a Country distinguished from the rest of the World, by being a Government of Laws, where Liberty has found a safe and secure abode, and where her sons are determined to support and protect her.

"Brethren we are called this day by our honorable & patriotic Governor, his Excellency Samuel Adams to assist him in laying the cornerstone of a building to be erected for the use of the Legislative and Executive branches of Government of this Commonwealth. May we, my Brethren, so square our actions thro life as to show to the World of Mankind, that we mean to live within the compass of Good Citizens, that we wish to stand upon a level with them, that when we part we may be admitted to the Temple where Reigns Silence and Peace."

Underneath this corner-stone was placed a silver plate bearing the following inscription:

"This Corner Stone of a Building, intended for the use of the Legislative and Executive branches of the
GOVERNMENT
"of the
"Commonwealth of MASSACHUSETTS
"was laid by
"His Excellency SAMUEL ADAMS, Esq.,
"Governor of said Commonwealth,
"Assisted by the Most Worshipful PAUL REVERE, Grand Master, and the Right-Worshipful WILLIAM SCOLLAY, Deputy Grand Master, The Grand Wardens and Brethren of the GRAND LODGES of MASONS, on the FOURTH Day of JULY AN. DOM. 1795. A. L. 5795.
"Being the xxth Anniversary of American Independence."

At the conclusion of the services, the Governor, amid the cheers of the multitude and the booming of cannon, was escorted to the Council Chamber.

Washington's Golden Urn Fashioned by Paul Revere

When Washington retired from the Presidency to the enjoyment of domestic life at Mount Vernon, the Grand Lodge of Massachusetts sent him the following address:

"The East, the West, and the South, of the Grand Lodge of Ancient and Accepted Masons for the Commonwealth of Massachusetts, to their most worthy Brother GEORGE WASHINGTON.

"Wishing ever to be foremost in testimonials of respect and admiration of those virtues and services with which you have so long adorned and benefited our common country, and not the last nor least to regret the cessation of them in the public councils of the Union, your brethren of this Grand Lodge embrace the earliest opportunity of greeting you in the calm retirement you have contemplated to yourself.

"Though as citizens they lose you in the active labors of political life, they hope as Masons to find you in the pleasing sphere of fraternal engagement. From the cares of State, and the fatigues of public business our institution opens a recess, affording all the relief of tranquility, the harmony of peace, and the refreshment of pleasure. Of these may you partake in all their purity and satisfaction, and we will assure ourselves that your attachment to this social plan will encrease; and that, under the auspices of your encouragement, assistance, and patronage, the Craft will attain its highest ornament, perfection and praise. And it is our earnest prayer, that when your light shall be no more visible in this earthly Temple, you may be raised to the All Perfect Lodge above, be seated on the right of the

Supreme Architect of the Universe, and receive the refreshment your labors have merited.

"In the behalf of the Grand Lodge, we subscribe ourselves, with the highest esteem, your affectionate brethren,

"PAUL REVERE, *Grand Master.*
"ISAIAH THOMAS, *Senior Grand Warden.*
"JOSEPH LAUGHTON, *Junior Grand Warden.*
"DANIEL OLIVER, *Grand Secretary.*
"Boston, March 21, 5797."

To this address Washington replied in a letter filled with kind and reciprocal sentiments. On the death of Washington the Masonic Fraternity in Boston, took prominent and appropriate action. A special meeting of the Grand Lodge of Massachusetts was held in Concert Hall,2 January 8, 1800, to make the necessary preparations for the "commemoration of the decease of our late Illustrious Brother, George Washington!" A vote was passed to form a public procession on the 11th of February, and invite all the Lodges under the jurisdiction of the Grand Lodge to participate.

A committee was appointed to make arrangements for the delivery of a "Funeral Oration or Eulogium" on Washington. This oration was delivered by Timothy Bigelow, and it was afterwards printed in both pamphlet and book.

Still another committee of the Grand Lodge was appointed, consisting of "R. W. Brothers John Warren, Paul Revere and Josiah Bartlett, Past Grand Masters," to write a letter of condolence to Mrs. Washington and to request a lock of hair to be placed in a golden urn crafted by Paul Revere.

This "golden urn" is three and seven-eights inches high, and was made by Paul Revere, as was also, without doubt, the wooden pedestal on which it stands, which has a door with lock and key, and into which the urn is placed when unscrewed from its resting place on the top. It has this inscription:

"This Urn incloses a Lock of Hair of the Immortal WASHINGTON, Presented, January 27, 1800, to the MASSACHUSETTS GRAND LODGE, by HIS amiable WIDOW. Born Feb. 11, 1732. Ob^t. Decr. 14, 1799."

Golden Urn with Washington's Hair

The top unfastens and the lock of hair is coiled under glass. This precious relic is jealously and sacredly guarded, being handed down from one Grand Master to another out of whose possession it never passes. A companion urn has recently been obtained by the Grand Lodge, which contains a lock of hair belonging to James Abram Garfield. The funeral solemnities of Washington, were observed in Boston, February 12, 1800, under the auspices of the Masonic Fraternity, on which occasion Revere was one of the Pallbearers. The insignia consisted of a pedestal covered with a pall on which was a large white marble urn, and other suitable emblems. On the urn was the inscription: "Sacred to the Memory of Brother George Washington; raised to the ALL PERFECT LODGE Dec.

14, 5799. — Ripe in years and full of glory." For many years this urn was sacredly cared for. On the 13th of March, 1809, the Masons appointed a committee to "examine the Urn &c. procured by the Grand Lodge as a testimony of their Veneration for the exalted character, and example of their Illustrious Brother, and Patron, George Washington, Esq. Deceased; and to enquire if a suitable place could be appropriated for it in Mason's Hall." That committee reported that they had visited the House of R. W. Paul Revere Esq. Past Grand Master, and find that the most scrupulous care had been observed in the preservation of the Urn and its appendages: They also find that the most proper place for them in the Hall is directly over the Chair of the M. W. Grand Master; and the following communication was sent at this time:

Boston, March 15, 1809.
"R. W. Paul Revere, ESQ.
"The following Resolve passed the Grand Lodge the last quarterly Communication, I with pleasure transmit you ; also our last printed Circular and remain with great personal respect and Brotherly affection yours,
"JOHN PROCTOR - G^d *Secretary.*

"Resolved — that the thanks of the Grand Lodge be given to the Right W. Paul Revere Esq Past Grand Master, for the care he has hitherto taken of the Urn & its appendages, used at the Funeral procession of our Most Worthy and Revered R. W. Brother George Washington Esq. Deceased; and that he be requested to permit them to remain under his protection, until the Grand Lodge shall have it in their power otherwise to dispose of them.
"Attest JOHN PROCTOR
G. Secy."

Benjamin Franklin

The name of Benjamin Franklin illumines the history of Masonry, and of our country, for more than one-half of the last century. Its diamond light is not confined to the city, the province, or the country that gave him birth. The orient borrows a ray from it, and wherever the evening twilight lingers, or the polar-star guides, or the southern-cross gleams, there the torch which he lighted from the clouds above him, irradiates the pathway still of every civilized nation. Of his humble birth in Boston, on the 17th of January, 1706; of his early employment in an occupation unsuited to his genius; of his being indentured to his brother as a printer's apprentice, and fleeing from his petty tyranny to Philadelphia; of his amusing introduction to that city, and his boyhood success there; of his leaving it for a voyage to London while he was yet in his minority, and of his first London life; every step from tottering infancy to bold reliant manhood, has been often told, and we need not repeat them in our sketch of his Masonic life.

Leaving the youth of Franklin with all its romantic incidents and instructive lessons behind us, we find him on his return from England in the autumn of 1726, in his twenty-first year, recommencing his citizenship in Philadelphia, with a body strong and vigorous, a mind active and well cultivated, and with a knowledge of his art, and an experience gained in the school of the world, which well fitted him to step boldly on to the platform of active life. His intentions at this period were to fit himself for a mercantile life, but the death of his employer soon induced him to engage again as a printer, and his industry, integrity, and studious habits soon gained him friends, competence, and distinction.

His social qualities and intelligence at first drew around him a few congenial spirits, and a literary club was formed for mental improvement. While in London he had become familiar with the existence of the various clubs and other social societies that existed there, and the organization of Freemasonry had no doubt come under his observation. This institution there was then just emerging from a situation which the common observer might have regarded as a system of voluntary social clubs, and its pretentious to antiquity, its moral and scientific basis, and its written rules and regulations, had lately been given to the public in a quarto volume called "Anderson's Constitutions." These had been accepted there by a part of the Fraternity as their governing code of rules, while others still adhered to the immemorial rights and usages of Masons when convened. There can be very little doubt but that Franklin brought home with him some knowledge of the Fraternity, although not an initiate into its mysteries.

As the limits of this sketch will not allow a detail of all the incidents of Franklin's private and public life, however interesting and instructive they may be, we shall pass over many of them, and confine our consideration more to those which show his character as a Mason, and the influence which his connection with this fraternity may have had on his afterlife. This we do more especially from believing that all which concerns the personal history of our representative men, should be fairly considered 'as a part of our national character, and from a belief that the Masonic character and connection of our public men of the last century, has been unwarrantably lost sight of, in the history of our country. Perhaps this has arisen from an undue prejudice which writers may have had against the institution of Freemasonry, or from an ignorance of its principles and influence.

With Franklin, whatever induced scientific research, and strengthened the fraternal bonds that thus bound society together, had especial value; and when he found that Freemasonry embraced in its teachings the highest moral rectitude, founded on the Fatherhood of God as a common parent, and the brotherhood of man as His offspring, and that it inculcated a study of His perfections as revealed in the works of nature as well as in His written word, he at once became a devotee at its altar. No record has come down to us of the time and place where he first received Masonic light. It was not the custom of the Fraternity in the early part of the last century to preserve written records of its meetings when convened for work; besides, when warranted lodges were first established in America, they little knew how much interest would in time be felt in their early history. The brief records they may have written, have in many cases, too, been destroyed or lost. It is not known how or when the first lodge of Freemasons was instituted in Philadelphia. A few brethren who had been made Masons in the old country, may have met and opened lodges from time to time, and initiated others, without keeping any record. The earliest notices we find of Masonic lodges in that city, are in the public newspapers of that day, which show the meetings of the Fraternity there in 1732, where they give the name of William Allen, the Recorder of the city, as their Grand Master. They met at that time at the "Tun Tavern;" and one of the lodges in Philadelphia was formerly called *Tun Lodge*, in allusion to the place of its early meetings.

Tun Tavern

The Society of the Free and Easy

There is no known record of Franklin's being a member of the Fraternity previous to this; but in 1732 he was Senior Warden under William Allen. In his own personal narrative he gives his written observations, in May, 1731, in which he says:

"There seems to me at present to be great occasion for raising a *United Party for Virtue*, by forming the virtuous and good men of all nations into a regular body, to be governed by suitable, good, and wise rules, which good and wise men may probably be more unanimous in their obedience to, than common people are to common laws. I at present think, that whoever attempts this aright, and is well qualified, cannot fail of pleasing God, and of meeting with success."

He has also left us a record of what he believed should be the fundamental principles of such a union or society, which he reduced to six heads viz.:

"That there is one God, who made all things.
"That He governs the world by His providence.
"That He ought to be worshipped by adoration, prayer, and thanksgiving.
"But that the most acceptable service to God is doing good to man.
"That the soul is immortal.
"And that God will certainly reward virtue and punish vice, either here or hereafter."

It is a matter of curious speculation rather than of certainty, whether Franklin drew this epitome of the great moral governing principles of Freemasonry from his own reflections, or had been taught them in a lodge of the craft. If the former, he was certainly prepared *in his heart* to be a Mason: if the latter, he either believed that to be a Mason, required in addition to these, a greater attention to the arts and sciences than all good men were disposed to give; or he believed that an organization, semi-masonic, might be beneficial, in which the initiates might first be schooled in the moral principles of Masonry, before they were admitted to its mysteries; for he proposed at that time to form a secret club, to be called THE SOCIETY OF THE FREE AND EASY. This, he says, he communicated in part to two of his companions, who adopted it with some enthusiasm; but his multifarious public and private engagements so occupied his time, that it was postponed, and finally abandoned.

We pass over three years more of Franklin's life, during which he was engaged as a printer and stationer and in which he commenced the publication of his *Poor Richard's Almanac* and find him receiving a written warrant from Henry Price, Provincial Grand Master of Massachusetts, constituting him Master of the Lodge, and probably of all the Masons in Philadelphia. The exact date of this authority from Price cannot be given. Massachusetts authorities say it was June 24th, 1734, while Pennsylvania authorities say that on that day the brethren in Philadelphia celebrated the festival of St. John the Baptist, under their old organization, and having accepted the authority of St. John's Grand Lodge at Boston, they ratified the choice of Franklin as their Master (or *Grand Master,* as they chose to term him). This apparent discrepancy in the date of Franklin's authority from Price, and his commencing his official duties under it in Philadelphia, both being given as the same day, probably arose from Price having granted to

Franklin a deputation previous to the 24th of June, and that at the festival which was held simultaneously in Boston and Philadelphia on that day, the act of Price was ratified by the Grand Lodge at Boston, and Franklin's commission accepted by the brethren assembled in Philadelphia.

The Masonic Fraternity was not so novel at this time in Philadelphia, nor its members so obscure as to be unknown or unnoticed; for at the festival of St. John the Baptist, in 1734, when Franklin's commission was accepted, and at the one which had been held on the same day the year before, the governor of the province, the mayor of the city, and many other distinguished citizens were present as members or guests. Franklin on this occasion appointed John Carp his Deputy, and James Hamilton and Thomas Hopkinson his Wardens. There is no doubt but that for some years previous to this the Masons in Philadelphia had been organized as a body, holding annually their festivals and electing their Grand Master without written authority from the ruling Grand Lodge of England or any of its dependencies, but by virtue of what had been deemed the immemorial right of Masons. Through Franklin they may have learned of the new regulations of the Order, and they perhaps instructed him to take such measures as would justify them before the world in the regularity of their organization. They had virtually existed as a Grand Lodge previous to Franklin's commission, and under it they no doubt exercised all the prerogatives, and assumed the dignity of a Grand Body. The claim, therefore, that Franklin was the first Master, or the first Grand Master in Pennsylvania, can only mean that he was so by authority derived from the Grand Lodge at London, which had, in 1721, assumed authority over all lodges of Masons.

Printing of the First American Constitution of Freemasonry

From the correspondence which took place between Franklin and the Grand Master and the brethren in Boston, soon after he became connected with their authority, we give the following letters of his which have been preserved:

"RIGHT WORSHIPFUL GRAND MASTER, AND MOST WORTHY AND DEAR BRETHREN—We acknowledge your favor of the 23d of October past, and rejoice that the Grand Master (whom God bless) hath so happily recovered from his late indisposition, and we now (glass in hand) drink to the establishment of his health, and the prosperity of your whole Lodge.

"We have seen in the Boston prints an article of news from London, importing, that at a Grand Lodge held there in August last, Mr. Price's deputation and power was extended over all America, which advice we hope is true, and we heartily congratulate him thereupon. And though this has not as yet been regularly signified to us by you, yet, giving credit thereto, we think it our duty to lay before your Lodge what we apprehend needful to be done for us, in order to promote and strengthen the interests of Masonry in this province (which seems to want the sanction of some authority derived from home, to give the proceedings and determinations of our Lodge their due weight); to wit: a Deputation or Charter, granted by the Eight Worshipful Mr. Price, by, virtue of his commission from Britain, confirming the brethren of Pennsylvania in the privileges they at present enjoy, of holding annually their Grand Lodge, choosing their Grand Master, Wardens, and other officers who may manage all affairs relating to the brethren here, with full power and authority according' to the customs and usages of Masons, the said Grand Master of Pennsylvania only yielding his chair when the Grand Master of all America shall be in place. This, if it seem good and reasonable to you to grant, will not only be extremely agreeable to us, but will also, we are confident, conduce much to the welfare, establishment, and reputation of Masonry in these parts. We therefore submit it to your consideration; 'and as we hope our request will be complied with, we desire that it may be done as soon as possible, and also accompanied with a copy of the Right Worshipful Grand Master's first Deputation, and of the instrument by which it appears to be enlarged, as above mentioned, witnessed by your Wardens, and signed by the secretary, for which favor this Lodge doubt not of being able to behave as not to be thought ungrateful.

"We are, Right Worshipful Grand Master, and Most Worthy Brethren, your affectionate brethren and obliged humble servants,

"B. Franklin, G. M.

"Signed at the request of the Lodge.
"Philadelphia, November 28, 1734."

Franklin sent with this letter to the Grand Lodge of Massachusetts, the following private note to Mr. Price the Grand Master:

"DEAR BROTHER PRICE—I am heartily glad to hear of your recovery. I hoped to have seen you here this fall, agreeable to the expectation you were so good as to give me; but, since sickness has prevented your coming while the weather was moderate, I have no room to flatter myself with a visit from you before spring, when a deputation from the Brethren here will have an opportunity of showing how much they esteem you. I beg leave to recommend their request to you, and to inform you that some false and rebel brethren, who are foreigners, being about to set up a distinct Lodge, in opposition to the old and true brethren here, pretending to make Masons for a bowl of punch; and the Craft is like to come into disesteem among us, unless the true brethren are countenanced and distinguished by some such special authority as herein desired. I entreat, therefore, that whatever you shall think proper to do therein, may be sent by the next post, if possible, or the next following.

"I am your affectionate brother and humble servant,

"B. Franklin, G. M. of Pennsylvania.

"P. S. If more of the Constitutions are wanted among you, please hint it to me."

The *Constitutions* here alluded to, were a reprint of the English Constitutions of Masonry, which had been collated and published in London in 1723. An American edition of this work was printed by Franklin in Philadelphia, in 1734, and it was the first Masonic book ever published in America. It was a small quarto volume, and a few copies still exist in antiquarian collections.

Franklin was at this time twenty-eight years of age; and while he diligently pursued his business as a printer and stationer, he also devoted his spare moments to the acquisition of useful knowledge. He was not a recluse, and he associated with him in his literary pursuits a few young men of studious habits and congenial tastes, who formed a club they called the *Junto*. The governing rules of this club have been incorporated into the Philosophical Society of Philadelphia; and the collection of books they formed, was the nucleus of the present magnificent library of that city.

Burning of Young Man in Farce Masonic Ceremony

In 1735, Franklin was superseded in his position as Master, or Grand Master as it was termed, by James Hamilton his Senior Warden, who was elected in his stead. Freemasonry in Philadelphia, although it appears to have been popular at this time, was soon after under the ban of public suspicion there, and Franklin's connection with it was much commented on by the public press of that city. It appears from the civil records and public journals of that day, that in 1737 a few thoughtless individuals attempted to impose on an ignorant young man and persuade him that by submitting to some ridiculous ceremonies he might become a Mason. He submitted to all they required, and was by them invested with sundry pretended Masonic signs, and told he had taken the first degree.

The principal perpetrators of the farce appear not to have been Masons, but they soon after communicated to Franklin and others an account of their practical joke, and told him they might expect to be saluted with the signs they had given to the young man when they met him. Franklin did not approve of their imposition, but laughed heartily at the ridiculous farce they had played, and thought no more of it. Not so with the active parties in it; for they determined to farther dupe the young man, and for this purpose induced him to take a second degree, in which they blindfolded and conducted him into a dark cellar, where one of the party was to exhibit himself to him disguised in a bull's hide, the head and horns of which were intended to represent the devil; while the others were to play a game they called snap-dragon, which consisted of picking raisins from a dish of burning fluid. When the bandage was taken from the young man's eyes, and he had gazed for a moment on the scene before him, one of the party thoughtlessly threw upon him the pan of burning fluid, which set fire to his clothes, and so burned him that he lingered for but three days and then died. This occurrence caused great excitement in Philadelphia, and the guilty parties were arrested and punished for manslaughter.

As it appeared at the judicial investigation, that Franklin had been made acquainted with the first outrage on the young man after its perpetration, although he had no knowledge that a second attempt was to be made, and disapproved of the first, many ignorant or excited citizens, knowing his Masonic position, sought to cast odium on him and the Fraternity of which he was a leading member.

A personal attack was also made on the character of Franklin by a newspaper in Philadelphia, accusing him of conniving at the outrage. This was promptly denied by him, and the denial was verified by the oaths of those who were acquainted with the whole affair. The Grand Lodge also deemed it its duty to express its disapprobation of such proceedings, and the Grand Officers appeared before the authorities in Philadelphia and signed the following declaration:

"*Pennsylvania, ss.*—Whereas some ill-disposed persons in this city, assuming the names of Freemasons, have, for some years past, imposed upon several well-meaning people who were desirous of becoming true brethren, persuading them, after they had performed certain ridiculous ceremonies, that they had really become Freemasons; and have lately, under the pretence of making a young man a Mason, caused his death by purging, vomiting, burning, and the terror of certain diabolical, horrid rites; it is therefore thought proper, for preventing such impositions for the future, and to avoid any unjust aspersions that may be thrown on this ancient and honorable Fraternity on this account, either in this city or any other part of the world, to publish this advertisement declaring the abhorrence of all true brethren of such practices in general, and their ignorance of this fact in particular, and that the persons concerned in this wicked action are not of our society, nor of any society of Free and Accepted Masons, to our knowledge or belief.

"Signed in behalf of all the members of St. John's Lodge in Philadelphia, 10th day of June, 1737.

"Thos. Hopkinson, G. Master.
"Wm. Plumstead, D. G. Master.
"Jos. Shippen, Warden
"Henry Pratt, Warden."

The knowledge of the outrage that had been perpetrated in Philadelphia in the name of Freemasonry, and the attack on Franklin's character, soon came to his parents in Boston, and his mother, with true maternal feelings, induced his father to write to him on the subject, and make inquiries respecting the society which was then agitating the public mind. To these inquiries Franklin replied under date of April 13th, 1738:

"As to the Freemasons, I know of no way of giving my mother a better account of them than she seems to have at present; since it is not allowed that women should be admitted into that secret society. She has, I must confess, on that account, some reason to be displeased with it; but for any thing else, I must entreat her to suspend her judgment till she is better informed, unless she will believe me when I assure her, that they are in general a very harmless sort of people, and have no principles or practices that are inconsistent with religion and good manners."

Although the excitement had run so high in Philadelphia, that during the trial of those who had been engaged in duping the young man with pretended Masonic degrees, every Mason was challenged from the jury-box, yet Franklin's popularity did not suffer. He was then postmaster of the city, and clerk of the Provincial Assembly, and he continued to hold these offices for many years. In 1747 he was elected a member of the Assembly, and held the office by reelection for ten years. In 1749 the old authority from Henry Price to Franklin in 1734 was superseded by a new warrant to him from Thomas Oxnard, Provincial Grand Master of all North America, constituting him Provincial Grand Master of Pennsylvania, with power to charter new Lodges. On the 5th of September of this year, Franklin accordingly convened the brethren by virtue of his new authority, and appointed Dr. Thomas Bond, Deputy Grand Master; Joseph Shippen and Philip Syng, Grand Wardens; William Plumstead, Grand Treasurer; and Daniel Byles, Grand Secretary. The following year Franklin was succeeded as Grand Master by William Allen, the Recorder of the City of Philadelphia, who was commissioned direct by the Grand Master of England.

Franklin at this time was deeply absorbed in philosophical investigations, and soon after was able to verify his belief that the lightning and thunder of the summer cloud were but electrical phenomena. The story of his drawing down the lightning with his kite is well known; and the discovery he thereby made has rendered his name immortal in the annals of science. He was well known at this period as the friend and patron of popular education and every useful art. It was not apathy and indifference on the part of the community respecting education that he had to contend with alone; but there was an element in the population of Philadelphia and its vicinity that regarded all measures for the greater diffusion of knowledge, as dangerous innovations on the established customs of society. There still exists a correspondence between one Christopher Sowrs, a German printer in Germantown, and Conrad Weiser, in which the former complains bitterly of the efforts of Franklin and the Freemasons generally to establish free schools. He says:

"The people who are the promoters of the *free* schools, are *Grand Masters* and *Wardens* among the Freemasons, their very pillars."

The loss of old Masonic records makes it impossible to determine the lodge membership in Philadelphia at this time, but enough remains to show that it embraced the first men in the city.

At the middle of the last century, Franklin had reached the meridian of his life, being forty-four years of age; but the sun of his fame was still in the ascendant, and from that period onward until it passed from our sight in a glowing west, its blaze seemed brighter and fuller. From the time when he was first seen a forlorn boy in the streets of Philadelphia, he had been steadily gaining strength of mind and public confidence, until his services were almost exclusively claimed by his fellow-citizens. In 1753 he was appointed deputy postmaster of all the British colonies in America, and the same year a commissioner to negotiate a treaty with the Indians. In 1754 he was a delegate to the Congress that met at Albany to devise means of defence against the French; and in this body his wisdom and sagacity were seen in the recommendation which he made of a Union of the colonies. He rendered important aid to the British commanders in the early part of the old French war, but was soon after sent to England as the agent of Pennsylvania and other colonies. There he was greatly caressed and distinguished, and found his situation widely different from what it was when he entered London a few years before, a poor journeyman printer: for now he was admitted into the presence of kings; and the Universities of Edinburg and Oxford conferred on him the degree of Doctor of Laws as a mark of their appreciation of his scientific attainments. This literary degree was not the first he had received; for the college at Cambridge, in Massachusetts, had before conferred on him the degree of Master of Arts. He also, while in London, visited the Grand Lodge of England; and its records show that he was honored with the rank of Provincial Grand Master on his visit to that body.

He returned to America in 1762, and resumed his seat in the Provincial Assembly of Pennsylvania, but two years afterwards he was sent again as their agent to England. He remained there until 1775. It was during this period that the disputes between the colonies and the mother country assumed their utmost seriousness, and his task was a difficult and delicate one; but so faithfully did he perform it, that on his return, he was elected a delegate from Pennsylvania to the Continental Congress, and the following year had the honor of signing the Declaration of Independence. During the whole period of the Revolution he was continually active in some civil capacity, either at home or abroad. Congress sent him in 1776 a commissioner to the court of France, and no diplomatist at Versailles was able to perform his duties with greater ability. He was well known in France at that time for his varied scientific attainments, and his plain republican manners rendered him a dignitary of a new light.

French Masonic Medal
and
Last Days

His residence was continued in France until 1785, and during this time he held intimate Masonic intercourse with the Masons of that country, and became affiliated, either as a special or honorary member, with the Grand Orient of France. He was also presented by his French brethren with a medal, of which the following description is given:

"Diameter one inch and three-fifths. Obverse Fine bust of FRANKLIN. Legend—'BENJAMIN FRANKLIN.' Reverse—Masonic emblems, the serpent's ring, carpenter's square and compass; in the centre a triangle and the sacred Name in Hebrew, &c. Legend—Leo. Mac. Fran, a Franklin. M: de la L—des 9 Soeurs O. de Paris, 5778."

When in 1785 he had fulfilled all the public duties which his country required of him in Europe, and was about to return to America, his Masonic brethren in France bade him a tender adieu, particularly the lodge at Rouen. When he arrived in Philadelphia he was received by his fellow-citizens with public testimonials of their gratitude and respect, and was soon afterwards elected to the chief executive office in Pennsylvania. He was then in his eightieth year, and might well have claimed a rest from his public labors; but he still continued for three years to give all his strength of body and mind to secure the fabric of liberty he had helped to erect. For this purpose, in 1787 lie permitted himself to be elected a member of the convention that framed the Federal Constitution, and his master hand gave to that instrument many of its provisions.

Franklin's official life closed in 1788, for his great age and infirmities rendered him unable to longer serve his country in a public capacity; but amid much suffering he survived for two more years, and died at Philadelphia on the 17th of April, 1790, in the eighty-fifth year of his age. He was buried on the 21st, in Christ Church yard in that city, and more than twenty thousand persons, it was said, attended the funeral. The highest dignitaries of the State were present on the occasion, and both the State and National Government decreed that badges should be worn in token of the loss all had sustained in the death of so great a man. It has been asked why so distinguished a Mason as Franklin was not interred with Masonic rites. The reader will remember that his Masonic connection in Philadelphia had been with the so-called Moderns, whose organization there had been superseded, during the absence of Franklin in Europe, by another denomination of Masons, called Ancients; and at his death, the Grand Lodge of which he had been the Grand Master was extinct. His name, however, and his virtues, have ever been kept in high veneration by Masons throughout the world, and with that of Washington are household words wherever the Craft is found.

John Sullivan, LL, D.

John Sullivan, the first Grand Master of Masons in New Hampshire, was of Irish descent. His father emigrated from Ireland to this country and settled in Berwick, in Maine, a few years before his birth. There, on the 17th of February, 1740, the subject of our sketch was born. He was his father's oldest son, and his early years were spent in assisting him upon his farm. When he came to manhood he studied law, and was regularly admitted by the court as an attorney. He established himself in his profession in Durham, New Hampshire, and soon rose to distinction as an attorney and politician. In 1774 he was sent as a delegate from New Hampshire to the Continental Congress. On his return home, he was engaged with some other distinguished patriots of his State in taking possession of the British fort in the harbor of Portsmouth. It was a bold act, and one hundred barrels of powder and a quantity of cannon and small-arms were secured for the future use of the colonists by the transaction.

He was re-elected to Congress the following year, and remained in it until his services were required in his own State, when he returned home with a commission as one of the eight brigadier-generals which Congress appointed, and soon after repaired to Washington's headquarters at Cambridge. When the Continental army was organized in 1776, he was promoted to the rank of major-general, and was sent to take the command of troops in Canada. He was not successful in this expedition; was superseded in command of the northern division by General Gates, and joined the army of Washington at New York. Here the illness of General Greene placed him in command of his division at the battle of Brooklyn, in which he was taken prisoner. Being soon after exchanged for General Prescott, he again joined the army, and was placed in command of one of its four divisions. He was with Washington at the battles of Brandywine and Germantown, but while the army was quartered the following winter at Valley Forge, lie was sent to Rhode Island to take command of the troops stationed in that State. In the summer of 1778 he besieged the British force at Newport; but the want of the desired cooperation of the French fleet prevented his full success.

While in command in Rhode Island in the autumn of 1778, our first Masonic record relating to General Sullivan as a Mason appears. It was the permission granted by him to the Brethren under his command to join in the Masonic Festival of St. John, on the 28th of December of that year, in Providence. General Varnum, who was also stationed in Rhode Island, delivered the Masonic address that day.

General Sullivan had doubtless been made a Mason previous to the Revolution, but we have seen no record of the time or place. In the spring of 1779 he was called into a new field of operations, being sent in command of the expedition against the Indians and Tories of New York. In this service he was accompanied by General Clinton, and Colonel Proctor with his regiment of Pennsylvania artillery, in which a Military Lodge had recently been organized under Colonel Proctor as Master.

This expedition, successful in its designs but tragic in its events, was a distinct feature in the war of the Revolution; and the pages of our country's history have invested with a kind of romance the details of its progress and consummation. From the commencement of the war, the loyalists of the north had been joined with the Indians of the Six Nations in New York in cruel and destructive warfare on our northwestern borders. In Canada and along the mighty lakes and rivers of the north were British fortresses, in whose strongholds the loyalists found safe retreat and shelter from danger; and between these and the settlements and towns of the States which were in arms against the king, were the hunting-grounds and the war-paths of the Iroquois. Here, for years which they numbered by the leaves of their forest-trees, their old men and their women had rudely cultivated rich interval lands along the streams, and in many favorite places their cone-like cabins had clustered into villages. Around these the fruit-trees of their distant civilized neighbors had been planted and grown to maturity, and abundant cornfields supplied their wants when the fortunes of the chase failed them.

From these British fortresses upon the lakes, and the intervening wilderness fastnesses between them and the American settlements, the loyalists and Indians commingled together, and fell in predatory bands on many defenceless towns and villages, whose natural defenders were absent in the general defence of the country under Washington. Like arrows from an unseen bow, or fire-bolts from a mantling summer-cloud, they often came when and where they were least expected, and retired so quickly that no trace was left of them except the work of the firebrand and the hatchet, or the blood-stained footsteps of their captives in their hurried return to the wilderness of the Iroquois or the forts at Niagara. The forest domains of New York were a hiding-place for loyalists, and a storehouse and home to the Indians. The leaders of the loyalists were Sir John Johnson, Colonel Guy Johnson, and Colonels Butler and Claus, all relatives, and all formerly distinguished Masons of the Mohawk Valley, and members of St. Patrick's Lodge. Their Indian ally, Brant, the war-chief, was also a Mason. To him history has sometimes paid a tribute of respect for a remembrance of his Masonic vows during the bloody scenes of war, but to Johnson and Butler never. Their eyes had become blind to the Mason's sign, their ears deaf to the Mason's word. In the Masonic traditions of the Revolution, they have since stood as Ishmaelites in Israel. But let the mantle we seek to draw over our own faults, in part, cover theirs. History is not always impartial.

The expedition of General Sullivan in 1779 against these loyalists and Indians was a war measure, planned and approved by Washington as a punishment for the unjustifiable warfare of the allied loyalists and Indians; and by breaking up their strongholds and destroying their means of subsistence, to prevent their future depredations on our unprotected settlements. Sternly he gave what he deemed a necessary command, and most faithfully and severely did General Sullivan execute it. History has told it on its pages, and we have only space for some of its incidents.

WILDERNESS MARCH
&
MASONIC CEREMONIES

    Having no previous military road to use, General Sullivan was obliged to cut his pathway from Easton on the Delaware across a mountainous wilderness to Wyoming on the Susquehanna. As he approached the latter place, he sent a small advance company ahead under Captain Davis and Lieutenant Jones, They were met by a party of Indians, defeated, and the captain and lieutenant both slain and scalped. They were left by the Indians on the ground where they fell, and after their departure were hastily buried by their surviving comrades. Captain Davis and Lieutenant Jones were both Masons, and when General Sullivan reached the Valley, he had their bodies taken up and reinterred at "Wyoming with Masonic ceremonies."

    It was the first Masonic meeting ever held in that valley, and the procession of Brethren that bore the bodies of their slain companions from their first resting-place in the forest, for a more decent interment at Wyoming, was attended by the regimental band, which played Roslin Castle on their march. This Military Lodge, on that occasion, met at the marquee of Colonel Proctor. Neither history nor tradition has given us the names of Brethren present, but it is well known that a large number of the officers in that expedition were Masons, all of whom, whose duty permitted it, it is presumed, were present. The old town at Wyoming had, at that time, a few permanent inhabitants, whose descendants still reside there; and tradition of these events have the most positive verity.

Fifteen years later (1794) a Lodge was chartered in the same place by the Grand Lodge of Pennsylvania, which still exists as No. 61, at Wilkesbarre.

General Sullivan proceeded soon after on his expedition, following up the Susquehanna to its junction with the Tioga. Here, while awaiting the arrival of General Clinton who was to meet him with additional forces at this point, a Masonic funeral sermon on the death of Captain Davis and Lieutenant Jones was preached by Dr. Rodgers, one of the chaplains of the expedition. This service was held on the 18th of August, and the text was from the seventh verse of the seventh chapter of Job, "Remember that my life is wind." The progress of Masonry was thus following the footsteps of war in its advancement into the American wilderness. The sound of its gavel was renewed at old Tioga Point under a warrant granted by the Grand Lodge of Pennsylvania in 1796, for Lodge No. 70, which is still working but a few rods from where this Masonic sermon was preached in Fort Sullivan in 1779.

From the commencement of General Sullivan's wilderness march, the scouts of Brant and his Tory associates Johnson and Butler had watched his progress. They no doubt knew his design was to penetrate the heart of the Indian country, and perhaps proceed to Niagara. His superior numbers had now gained him an admission to their *House*, as they termed their country, the south-door of which they said was at "Tioga Point." There General Sullivan had been joined by two thousand men under General Clinton, making his number then five thousand.

With this strong force Brant, Johnson, and Butler saw General Sullivan enter the *south-door* of the Iroquois, and proceed up the Tioga. When near what was afterwards called Newtown (now Elmira), they laid an ambuscade and prepared to give him battle. His strength overcame their cunning and bravery, and defeated and disheartened they fell back before his victorious army, and saw him destroy their cornfields, cut down their orchards, and burn their towns without again offering a united resistance. One of the incidents of this devastating march is painfully interesting, and of a character entitling it to a place in Masonic narrative.

THE WARRING CONFLICT
OF TWO MASONS

After General Sullivan had passed into the heart of the Indian country, and was near the Genesee River, he sent Lieutenant Boyd with a guide and twenty-six men to reconnoiter an Indian town six miles ahead. His guide mistook the way, and on the return of the party, they were drawn into an ambuscade by Brant and Butler with several hundred Indians and rangers, as the loyalists were called, and nearly all his men were killed. Boyd was wounded, and with one of his party taken prisoner. He had been captured once before at the storming of Quebec, but then was exchanged. From the private ranks he had risen to that of lieutenant of a rifle company of the Pennsylvania division, and was about twenty-two years of age. He was the largest and most muscular man in his company, but having been wounded, he was now in the power of the enemy.

Lieutenant Boyd was a Mason, and knowing the ferocity of the Indians after seeing their towns burned, he gave to Brant, who was also a Mason, a sign of the Fraternity, claiming protection. The dusky chief recognized it and at once promised him his life. But being called away soon after, Boyd was left in the care of General Butler, who, as before stated, had formerly been a member of St. Patrick's Lodge on the Mohawk. Butler demanded of the captive information which his fidelity to his own commander would not allow him to give. The scene became one of tragic interest. Enraged at the silence of Boyd, Butler had him placed before him kneeling upon one knee, with an Indian on each side holding his arms, and another standing behind him with a tomahawk raised over his head. Butler inquired the number of Sullivan's men. "I cannot answer you," was Boyd's reply. He then inquired how his army was divided and disposed. "I cannot give you any information, sir," again replied the heroic captive. Again, for the third time, Butler harshly addressed him:

"Boyd, life is sweet; you had better answer me."

"Duty forbids," was the reply; "I would not, if life depended on the word."

Reader, contemplate the scene. Both were Masons; the one haughty, imperious, and forgetful of his vows; the other a captive in his hands, with fortitude undaunted and fidelity unshaken, thrice refusing to betray his trust. His last refusal cost him his life; for before Brant returned to his captive, and unknown to him, Butler delivered him into the hands of the infuriated Indians about him, and, amidst tortures too horrid to describe, he fell a martyr to his trust. Thus fell Lieutenant Boyd on the 13th of September, 1779. His remains were found on the following day, and buried by order of General Sullivan on the borders of a small stream, where they lay undisturbed until 1841, sixty-two years after the event, when they were identified, collected in an urn, and reinterred with much ceremony in Mount Hope Cemetery at Rochester.

General Sullivan proceeded no further on this expedition than the Indian towns on the Genesee, and returned to Tioga, still, burning wigwams, and destroying every means for subsistence within his reach. So dreadful and widespread was the devastation he made, that he was afterwards called by the Indians "The Town Destroyer." General Sullivan was absent from the headquarters of the army in this expedition about five months, and on his return received the thanks of Congress for his services; but he was dissatisfied with the action of the Board of War, pleaded ill-health, and resigned his commission in the army. He then retired to private life, and resumed his former profession. He was, however, immediately elected by the State of New Hampshire a delegate to Congress, and took his seat in that body in 1780. He left Congress after one year's service, and again returned to his profession. In 1783 he was appointed attorney-general of his State, helped to form its constitution, and was chosen a member of its council. In 1786 he was elected governor of New Hampshire, and hold the office for three successive years.

Sullivan Elected Grand Master

During the last year that General Sullivan occupied the gubernatorial chair of his State, an independent Grand Lodge was formed in that jurisdiction, and he was elected its first Grand Master. Masonic lodges were not numerous in New Hampshire at that time; but five having then been organized in the State, and but one of these (St. John's at Portsmouth) preceding the Revolution. During the same year that General Sullivan was Grand Master of the State, he was also Master of this old lodge at Portsmouth. In October of 1790, at a meeting of this Grand Lodge, General Sullivan communicated to that body by letter the fact, that the alarming state of his health would no longer permit him to serve as Grand Master, at the same time expressing his grateful acknowledgments for the honor they had conferred upon him. Dr. Hall Jackson was therefore elected Grand Master in his stead.

General Sullivan soon after received an appointment as Federal judge of his district, and held that office till the close of his life. He died on the 23d of January, 1795, in the fifty-sixth year of his age. Twenty years of his life had been spent in public service, but still he had found time to acquire a fund of general literature, and had been honored by the university at Dartmouth with the degree of Doctor of Laws. He led a life of usefulness, and his death was felt as a public loss.

Joseph Warren

Joseph Warren was initiated in St. Andrew's Lodge, of Boston, on the tenth of September, 1761. He received the second degree on the second of November following, but there is no record as to the third. On the fourteenth of November, 1765, the Lodge voted unanimously that Dr. Joseph Warren, be re-admitted a member of the Lodge. He was elected Master in 1769.

In December of the latter year, he received from the Earl of Dalhousie, Grand Master of Masons in Scotland, a commission, bearing date the thirtieth of May previous, appointing him Grand Master of Masons in Boston, and within one hundred miles of the same. In 1773, he received another commission, dated March 3, 1772, and signed by the Earl of Dumfries, then

Grand Master, extending his jurisdiction over the "Continent of America." He was installed under each of these commissions on the twenty-seventh of December of the respective years. Grand Master Warren presided over all the forty meetings of his Grand Lodge held previous to his death save four, namely, those of Dec. 27, 1770 (the Feast of St. John the Evangelist), June 16, 1773, June 3, and Sept. 2, 1774. On the last but one of these occasions, the record recites that the Grand Lodge "adjourned to Tuesday Evening Next, 7 o'clock; by reason of the few Grand Officers present; Engaged on Consequential Public Business."

On the first of June, 1774, Gen. Gage put in force the Boston Port Act, closing the harbor against all inward bound vessels, and on that day his predecessor, Ex-Governor Hutchinson, sailed for England. Great distress was caused by the sudden transformation of a busy, thriving town (whose inhabitants were mostly traders, shipwrights and sailors), into a scene of idleness and want. On the fifth of June, Joseph Warren reported to the Committee of Correspondence of the town of Boston a "Solemn League and Covenant" for the suspension of all commerce with the Island of Great Britain, until the repeal of the Port Act and the restoration of the charter rights of the Colony. Verily, the Brethren had "Consequential Business" on their hands about that time, and the Grand Master gave it his particular attention. He was present, however, at the adjourned meeting of the Grand Lodge, on the seventh of that month.

During the year 1760 he was employed as a teacher in a public school in Roxbury, and in the following year commenced the study of medicine under Dr, Lloyd, an eminent physician of that day, He began practice in 1703 and is said to have distinguished himself at once. In 1764, the small-pox prevailed extensively in Boston, and he was very successful in treating it. He thus gained the good will of the people and he never lost it. "His personal appearance, his address, his courtesy and his humanity, won the way to the hearts of all, and his knowledge and superiority of talents secured the conquest." About this time he began to take an active part in political affairs, and his letters to public men and newspaper essays soon attracted the attention even of the government. Considering his age, many of these productions are remarkable for clearness of thought, terseness of statement and cogency of argument.

Samuel Adams

He had caught the spirit and the style of Samuel Adams, the prime mover in the Revolution. The biographer of Adams says: "The bond of friendship and unreserved confidence was perfect between them, despite the difference in age," and Perez Morton, in his eulogy on Warren, declares that "their kindred souls were so closely twined, that both felt one joy, both one affliction. Warren was the closest friend that Samuel Adams ever had. No one among his younger associates in the cause, not even John Adams, ever enjoyed the confidence of Samuel Adams to such an extent as Warren, and that vacancy in his heart was never fully supplied In no letter of Samuel Adams can any allusion be found to the death of Warren. His sorrow was probably of that nature which could find no solace in writing or commenting upon his loss."

Continental Congress from Massachusetts, Warren was chosen to represent the town of Boston in the Provincial Congress, and in the following: year he was elected President of that Body. Here he manifested extraordinary powers of mind and a peculiar fitness for the guidance and government of men in times of difficulty and danger. "Cautious in proposing measures, he was assiduous in pursuing what he thought, after mature deliberation, to be right, and never counted the probable cost of a measure, when he had decided that it was necessary to be taken." The Congress was then sitting at Watertown, and it is said to have been his custom every day upon the adjournment to mount his horse and hurry off to the camp, there to participate with the common soldiers in the exercises and drill, and to encourage and animate them by exhortation and example. He thus became well known to most of the soldiers, and was readily recognized and welcomed by them when he made his appearance in their midst on the memorable seventeenth of June.

The Provincial Congress offered him the appointment of Surgeon General, but he declined it and accepted a commission as Major General dated only three days before the battle. He arrived upon the field only a few moments before the first attack of the British troops. This fact is accounted for by his nephew in a different manner from that heretofore received. In a recently published memoir of Dr. John Warren; Grand Master in 1783), the author says: "I have attended a lady who was born in Dedham on the seventeenth of June, 1775. Dr. Joseph Warren was engaged to attend her mother in her confinement. It is stated that he visited her on that morning, and finding she had no immediate occasion for his services, told her that he must go to Charlestown to get a shot at the British, and he would return to her in season. On the night of the sixteenth, it is well known that he presided at the meeting of the Colonial Congress, which continued in session a great part of the night in Watertown.

It is very probable that he returned to visit his mother and his children at Roxbury before the battle, and from there went to visit his patient. It is well known that he was late on the battle field. Of course he never returned to her again and she was attended by his pupil, Mr. Eustis. Thus it appears he was in active practice almost to the moment of his death." The story of the battle is familiar and also his share in it. His repeated refusal to take the command when offered it by Putnam and Prescott, his seizing a musket and flying from place to place wherever the fight was hottest, his reluctance to obey the order to retreat, being at only a few rods distance from the redoubt when the British had obtained full possession, his instant death by a bullet in the head, and his burial on the following day in a shallow grave beside the body of a butcher,—all these facts have been often recounted.

Masonic Monument to General Warren

Congress passed a resolution that a monument should be erected to his memory, and even prescribed the inscription, but it was never carried into effect. Immediately after the evacuation of Boston, his Brethren determined to go in search of the body. They repaired to the spot indicated by an eye-witness of his death. It was at the brow of the hill, and near the head of the grave was placed an acacia tree. Upon the removal of the earth, which appeared to have been recently disturbed, they indeed found the body of their Grand Master.

The remains were discovered on the sixth of April, 1776, carefully conveyed to the State House in Boston, and on the eighth of the same month were borne in solemn procession to King's Chapel, where an oration was delivered by Perez Morton, who was at that time Grand Marshal. His eulogy has often been compared to the oration of Mark Antony over the dead body of Caesar. The exordium was in these words:

"Illustrious relics! What tidings from the grave? Why hast thou left the peaceful mansions of the tomb, to visit again this troubled earth? Art thou the welcome messenger of peace? Art thou risen again to exhibit thy glorious wounds, and through them proclaim salvation to thy country? Or art thou come to demand that last debt of humanity to which your rank and merit have so justly entitled you, but which has been so long ungenerously withheld? And art thou angry at the barbarous usage? Be appeased, sweet ghost! for, though thy body has long laid undistinguished among the vulgar dead, scarce privileged with earth enough to hide it from the birds of prey—though not a kindred tear was dropped, though not a friendly sigh was uttered o'er thy grave—and though the execrations of an impious foe were all thy funeral knells—yet, matchless patriot! thy memory has been embalmed in the affections of thy grateful countrymen, who, in their breasts, have raised eternal monuments to thy bravery!

"But on none did he place so high a value as on that most honorable of all detached societies, the Free and Accepted Masons. Into this Fraternity he was early initiated, and after having given repeated proofs of a rapid proficiency in the art, and after having evidenced by his life the professions of his lips—finally, as the reward of his merit, he was commissioned the Most Worshipful Grand Master of all the Ancient Masons throughout North America. And you, Brethren, are living testimonies, with how much honor to himself and benefit to the Craft universal he discharged the duties of his elevated trust; with what sweetened accents he courted your attention, while, with wisdom, strength and beauty, he instructed his Lodges in the secret arts of Freemasonry; what perfect order and decorum he preserved in the government of them; and, in all his conduct, what a bright example he set us, to live within compass and act upon the square.

"With what pleasure did he silence the wants of poor and penniless Brethren; yea, the necessitous everywhere, though ignorant of the mysteries of the Craft, from his benefactions felt the happy effects of that Institution which is founded on Faith, Hope and Charity. And the world may cease to wonder that he so readily offered up his life on the altar of his country, when they are told that the main pillar of Masonry is the love of mankind." The fates, as though they would reveal in the person of our Grand Master those mysteries which have so long lain hid from the world, have suffered him, like the great master builder in the temple of old, to fall by the hands of ruffians and be again raised in honor and authority. We searched in the field for the murdered son of a widow, and we found him, by the turf and the twig, buried on the brow of a hill, though not in a decent grave. And though we must again commit his body to the tomb, yet our breasts shall be the burying spot of his Masonic virtues, and there 'An adamantine monument we'll rear, With this inscription—Masonry lies here.'"

After the funeral ceremonies, the remains were deposited in a tomb in the Granary Burying Ground, where they remained for nearly fifty years, and the place of deposit was forgotten.

As early as 1776, some steps were taken toward the commemoration of the Battle of Bunker Hill and the fall of General Warren, who was buried upon the hill the day after the action. The Massachusetts Lodge of Masons, over which Warren had presided, applied to the provisional government of Massachusetts for permission to take up his remains and to bury them with the usual solemnities. The council granted this request, on condition that it should be carried into effect in such a manner that the government of *the Colony* might have an opportunity to erect a monument to his memory. A funeral procession was had, and a eulogy on General Warren was delivered by Perez Morton, but no measures were taken toward building a monument.

A resolution was adopted by the Congress of the United States on the 8th of April, 1777, directing that monuments should be erected to the memory of General Warren, in Boston, and of General Mercer, at Fredericksburg; but this resolution has remained to the present time unexecuted.

On the 11th of November, 1794, a committee was appointed by King Solomon's Lodge, at Charlestown, to take measures for the erection of a monument to the memory of General Joseph Warren, at the expense of the lodge. This resolution was promptly carried into effect. The land for this purpose was presented to the lodge by the Hon. James Russell, of Charlestown, and it was dedicated with appropriate ceremonies on the 2d of December, 1794. It was a wooden pillar of the Tuscan order, eighteen feet in height, raised on a pedestal eight feet square, and of an elevation of ten feet from the ground. The pillar was surmounted by a gilt urn. An appropriate inscription was placed on the south side of the pedestal.

Masonic Monument in Memory of Grand Master General Joseph Warren

King Solomon's Lodge
&
The Bunker Hill Monument

In February, 1818, a committee of the legislature of Massachusetts was appointed to consider the expediency of building a monument of American marble to the memory of General Warren, but this proposal was not carried into effect.

As the half-century from the date of the battle drew toward a close, a stronger feeling of the duty of commemorating it began to be awakened in the community. Among those who from the first manifested the greatest interest in the subject was the late William Tudor, Esq. He expressed the wish, in a letter still preserved, to see upon the battleground "the noblest monument in the world," and he was so ardent and persevering in urging the project, that it has been stated that he first conceived the idea of it. The steps taken in execution of the project, from the earliest private conferences among the gentlemen first engaged in it to its final completion, are accurately sketched by Mr. Richard Frothingham, Jr., in his valuable *History of the Siege of Boston*. All the material facts contained in this note are derived from his chapter on the Bunker Hill Monument After giving an account of the organization of the society, the measures adopted for the collection of funds, and the deliberations on the form of the monument, Mr. Frothingham proceeds as follows:—

"It was at this stage of the enterprise that the directors proposed to lay the corner-stone of the monument, and ground was broken (June 7th) for this purpose. As a mark of respect to the liberality and patriotism of King Solomon's Lodge, they invited the Grand Master of the Grand Lodge of Massachusetts to perform the ceremony. They also invited General Lafayette to accompany the President of the Association, Hon. Daniel Webster, and assist in it.

"This celebration was unequalled in magnificence by anything of the kind that had been seen in New England. The morning proved propitious. The air was cool, the sky was clear, and timely showers the previous day had brightened the vesture of nature into its loveliest hue. Delighted thousands flocked into Boston to bear a part in the proceedings, or to witness the spectacle. At about ten o'clock a procession moved from the State House towards Bunker Hill. The military, in their fine uniforms, formed the van. About two hundred veterans of the Revolution, of whom forty were survivors of the battle, rode in barouches next to the escort. These venerable men, the relics of a past generation, with emaciated frames, tottering limbs, and trembling voices, constituted a touching spectacle. Some wore, as honorable decorations, their old fighting equipments, and some bore the scars of still more honorable wounds. Glistening eyes constituted their answer to the enthusiastic cheers of the grateful multitudes who lined their pathway and cheered their progress. To this patriot band succeeded the Bunker Hill Monument Association. Then the Masonic fraternity, in their splendid regalia, thousands in number. Then Lafayette, continually welcomed by tokens of love and gratitude, and the invited guests. Then a long array of societies, with their various badges and banners. It was a splendid procession, and of such length that the front nearly reached Charlestown Bridge ere the rear had left Boston Common. It proceeded to Breed's Hill, where the

Grand Master of the Freemasons, the President of the Monument Association, and General Lafayette performed the ceremony of laying the corner-stone, in the presence of a vast concourse of people."

Bunker Hill Monument

Index

A
Adam, Robert – 66, 67, 71, 131
Adams, John – 11, 99, 115, 117, 118, 166, 167, 187, 228
Adams, Nathaniel - 150
Adams, Samuel – 187, 188, 227, 228
Allen, William – 196, 197, 206

B
Bartlett, Josiah – 117, 148, 185, 190
Baynter, Peter - 36
Bigelow, Timothy – 149, 190
Bissell, Ozias – 15
Blagden, Thomas - 164
Blair, John – 17, 29
Brent, William - 164
Broeck, John - 145
Brooks, John - 55
Brown, Prentice – 25
Bruce, Stephen - 182

C
Carbery, Thomas – 160, 164
Carroll, Daniel – 81, 89, 175
Chapman, James - 15
Chase, Thomas - 13
Clark, Joel – 13, 15, 16
Clark, Peleg - 152
Clarke, Joseph – 86, 89, 90
Cleavland, William - 15
Coats, John – 20
Colden, Cadwalader - 145
Cornwallis, Charles – 46, 48, 56
Coxe, Daniel – 13, 14
Custis, George - 47
Custis, John – 47, 167, 168
Custis, Nelly – 47, 120

D
Davis, Thomas – 125, 126, 128, 129, 133, 135
Day, Benjamin - 153
Deneale, George – 126, 127, 131, 133

Dick, Elisha – 66, 83, 96, 124, 126, 129, 131, 133, 177
Dunn, Samuel – 117, 146

F
Fendall, Philip – 160, 164
Force, Peter - 160
Franklin, Benjamin – 13, 14, 59, 193-195, 197-207, 210, 211

G
Gist, Mordecai - 25
Gleason, Micajah - 15
Gore, Nathaniel – 15
Graham, Charles - 25
Gridley, Richard – 13, 117
Gustavus the Third - 61

H
Habt, Jonathan – 24
Hallate, Stephen - 89
Hamilton, James – 199, 203
Hancock, John – 11
Handy, John - 152
Harrison, George - 45
Hart, Jonathan – 13, 16, 25
Haskins, William - 38
Hays, Moses – 45
Henderson, Archibald - 164
Henry, Patrick – 11
Herbert, William – 71
Hoban, James – 89
Hoffman, Martin - 145
Hopkins, Elisha - 15
Hopkinson, Thomas – 199, 205
Houston, Sam - 167
Howe, John – 13
Hull, William – 22
Humphrey, David - 80

J
Jewett, Joseph - 15
Johnson, John – 16, 216, 218
Jones, Walter – 160, 164

Index

L
LaFayette, Marie-Joseph – 46, 51, 72-74, 155
Laughton, Joseph – 101, 117, 190
Lawrence, John - 25
Lear, Tobias – 124, 127, 143, 148
Lee, Henry – 138, 141
Lenox, Walter - 164
Lewis, Lawrence – 74, 119
Livingston, Robert – 73, 76, 77

M
Machin, Thomas - 25
Maffit, William – 128, 132, 135
Malcolm, William – 30
Mason, Williamson – 89
McCrea, Robert – 131
Mewell, Jonathan - 151
Mobbis, Gouverneub - 145
Morse, Jedediah - 119
Morton, Jacob – 143, 145
Morton, Perez – 182, 185, 227, 230, 232
Munroe, Thomas – 160, 164

O
Oliver, Daniel – 101, 117, 146, 190

P
Palfrey, William – 30, 32
Park, John – 13, 20
Parsons, Samuel - 13
Patterson, John 21, 22, 55
Petrekin, Thomas - 126
Pierce, John - 23
Plumstead, William – 205, 206
Polk, James – 160, 164
Proctor, Edward - 182
Proctor, John – 20, 30, 141, 182, 192, 215, 217
Proctor, Thomas - 141

R
Ramsey, William - 67
Randolph, Peyton – 9, 11, 12, 64
Revere, Paul – 15, 101, 148, 173, 179-185, 187-192
Revere, Jr., Paul - 182
Richards, George - 151

S
Sanford, John 25
Scott, Ezekial - 13
Scott, Robert – 46
Scott, Winfield - 160
Seabury, Samuel - 121
Shippen, Joseph – 205, 206
Skinner, Abraham - 145
Smith, Jonathan - 138
Smith, William – 19, 20, 31, 32, 36, 40, 41, 58
Steuart, David – 81, 82, 89, 175
Sullivan, John – 213, 214, 216-218, 220, 221, 223
Symington, Thomas - 166

T
Thomas, Isaiah – 101, 190
Tichneob, Isaac – 151
Townson, Nathan – 160, 164
Tudor, George - 25

V
Van Buren, Martin - 167

W
Warren, John – 148, 190
Warren, Joseph – 11, 21, 116, 117, 180-182
Washington, George – 9-12, 14-24, 27-31, 38-64, 66-81, 83-91, 94-105, 107-109, 111-114, 118-131, 133-135, 137-141, 143-153, 155, 156, 158, 160-163, 165, 167, 171, 173, 174, 189-192, 211, 214-216
Washington, Martha – 12, 47, 72, 124, 142, 143, 147, 148, 173, 190
Watterston, George – 160, 164
Watson, Elkanah – 52-54, 70, 72-74, 98, 155
Webb, Joseph – 17, 32, 180, 182
Webster, Daniel – 166, 235
Weems, Mason – 121-123
Whittlesey, Elisha – 159, 161
Williams, Ortho – 15, 25, 26
Winthrop, Robert – 166, 167
Wyllys, John - 15
Wyllys, Samuel - 13

List of Texts Consulted

George Washington and His Masonic Compeers, Sidney Hayden, 1869.

Washington's Masonic Correspondence as Found Among the Washington Papers in the Library of Congress, Julius F. Sachse, 1915.

History of the Washington National Monument and of the Washington National Monument Society, Frederick L. Harvey, 1902.

The History of the Bunker Hill Monument Monument Association During the First Century of the United States of America, George Washington Warren, 1877.

History of the Grand Lodge and of Freemasonry in the District of Columbia with Biographical Index, W. Bro. Kenton N. Harper, 1911.

The Book of the Ancient and Accepted Scottish Rite of Freemasonry Containing Instructions in All the Degrees From the Third to the Thirty-Third, and Last Degree of the Rite. Together with Ceremonies of Inauguration, Institution, Installation, Grand Visitations, Reflections, Lodges of Sorrow, Adoption, Constitutions, General Regulations, Calendar, Etc., Charles T. McClenachan, 1808.

The New England Freemason, Vol. I, Serenod D. Nickerson, A.M., 1874.

The life of Colonel Paul Revere, Elbridge Henry Goss, Vols. I & II, 1891, pgs. 465-498.

The History of Freemasonry in Canada from Its Introduction in 1749, J. Ross Robertson, Vol. I & II, 1900.

The Bunker Hill Monument Adams and Jefferson Two Orations by Daniel Webster with a Biographical Sketch and Brief Notes, Riverside Literature Series, December 1892.

Literature by Bottletree Classics
**Edgar Allan Poe Annotated and Illustrated
Entire Stories and Poems**

Tolstoy's 25 Greatest Short Stories Annotated

**Faust Parts I and II
Annotated and Illustrated**

Coffee with Poe

Orion: An Epic English Poem

Bottletree®

Great content. Great books.™

BottletreeBooks.com

www.ingramcontent.com/pod-product-compliance
Lightning Source LLC
Chambersburg PA
CBHW030314080526
44584CB00012B/571